An Awakening Perspective

My Journey To Conscious Evolution

Gary Hinebaugh

ISBN: 979-8-9869088-0-9

Printed in the United States of America

First Printing: September 2022

Library of Congress Number: 2022916803

Cover Design and Layout: Neha Hinebaugh

Disclaimer: Any guidance and information provided in this book is for your thoughtful consideration only. Gary Hinebaugh and Higher Dimensional Guidance & Healing LLC are not responsible for the reader's interpretation or decisions based on information provided. The reader accepts full personal and legal responsibility for their own life choices.

Published by Higher Dimensional Guidance & Healing LLC
www.higherdimensional.net

For Neha

My loving wife and Divine Partner

Without your support, love, and belief in me

I would never be who I am today

My gratitude is beyond words in

Past, present, and future lives

I love you more than you'll ever know

So much gratitude for all your support.

Tehune, Glad, My brother Mark

Thank you for sharing your journeys with me

My family, the rest of my Sedona family

Those who inspired and taught me

Pops… your words, clarity, and belief in me

Taught me to believe and trust in myself

Heal well, journey well…

Table of Contents

Foreword

Mankind is entering an age of great importance never experienced in our civilization. This shift into a global and universal Awakening is bringing many needed and necessary paradigm shifts, to better not only our quality of life, but our quality of spirit. As we are leaving behind the patriarchal societal rule of the Piscean age and entering the Divine Feminine Aquarian age, we begin a journey into balance. We will experience the restructuring of society, education, and beliefs brought by millennia of outdated thought, process, understanding, and control.

As we evolve, there will be a need to rise above all we were taught on every level from every institution of learning, meant for a time that no longer exists. There must be awareness brought to every spirit that the old ways of our society are not effective, and even more importantly, a more effective way that was discarded thousands of years ago already exists.

Many of the ancient beliefs written by bygone masters were destroyed in an attempt to control the population by means of fear. What they didn't realize is that truth cannot be destroyed. It is encoded in our DNA, passed down from our ancestors, and has been reactivated within the Awakening BEings among us today.

Higher Dimensional knowledge has always existed in Shamans, Druids, Seers, and every Holy BEing that ever walked this Earth, and is being remembered and spoken by many through their hearts. The corrupt societal leaders have persecuted and eradicated those who have spoken out to bring awareness to the masses of their controlling since the beginning of this civilization. They sought them out to silence their words to maintain control for their own personal agenda, without regard for human life or Mother Earth.

In this current time, however, we have a technology our ancestors didn't have to be able to communicate globally in an instant, spreading our message of Awakening. Unfortunately, the corrupt leaders also have the same technology to spread their fear and propaganda, so for now we exist within a new kind of power struggle and their disclaimers reach wide. Their control began to fade decades ago, and as our message of love spreads to the Newly Awakening, their iron fist of control decays, and the more they feel their grasp fade, the more they intensify their efforts. Global leaders exert their control, still today, by means of eradication, imprisonment, and even more deceitful and deadly ways than their predecessors.

Many Lightworkers, Wayshowers, and leaders of our revolution of millennia have given their lives, in their beliefs to bring the change necessary for the evolution of our species, and we should indeed honor those taken from us. As our "silent" revolution grows within the hearts of others, we will eventually experience an Event Horizon that will bring the change needed, once enough have become aware of their Awakening.

We all have our own journey with our own truth, but we all have a purpose within a larger scheme within the multiverse and a larger truth. Like apples on the tree, we come from the same source, but each is an individual, making our contribution to the overall experience of the Oneness, the Stream of Consciousness. Our contribution is to bring change within ourselves, healing emotionally, being love, and becoming our authentic selves.

Our mission as Awakening BEings is to not only spread awareness and become our authentic selves, it is to hold space for others as they become aware of their Awakening, helping each other evolve. What is meant by Awakening? There are many layers to many processes on our Awakening journey. It is a process, not an event, as many believe it to be.

Awakening means to be consciously aware of the self, existing in the moment and experiencing it without judgement, while allowing life to happen, living every aspect of our lives from the heart, and connecting to our own Divinity through becoming our authentic limitless selves... our spirit. It goes much deeper than all of this, and I will try to help in understanding and becoming an Awakening Being, while maintaining our 3D existence, and existing in another dimension as our spirit selves.

You have chosen to come here at this time for many reasons, in specific, because you chose to make your contribution, ensuring your own evolution and that of Mother Earth. This is the most important age in this civilization, as we join other galaxies and the multiverse in evolving and continuing the forward movement to enlightenment, rising above all limits and constructs in place since our introduction to this planet. You will always have free will — choice in how you conduct your existence — and you will be given the experiences necessary to grow and evolve, but there can be no denial of your purpose here. You wrote the story, signed the contract, and many other things before you came here.

Your existence is testimony to your ability to do what is necessary to evolve. Unfortunately, many will choose not to keep their promise and will walk away from their purpose, and that is your choice because it is your journey. There will be many words spoken in this book you will not agree with, and that's okay. You don't have to, as we all have our own truth, but please, if it resonates, allow yourself to act upon it. Intentions without action are merely words with no meaning.

My purpose in compiling these thoughts is to bring awareness and understanding to the Awakening process, and making sense of the many nuances within this complex existence. I am not teaching anything new to anyone, just helping your spirit to remember the lifetimes of knowledge you have within you, and bringing practical application to this process. I give gratitude to you for joining me and allowing me to share of myself as I follow my Divine Purpose, spreading awareness of the Awakening Process. Heal well, journey well.

Introduction

I invite you to join me on the adventure of my personal Awakening experiences and my life, not because I am an expert, but because my story is real. For some reason, I have been compelled to share my journey of conscious evolution, not to bring light to me as a person, but to help bring some understanding to our Awakening journey and how I perceive the processes within each and every one of us, and how I came to learn how to heal as I have. I live the very words I have brought to you, not as a concept, but a way of life.

I learned how to dedicate to becoming the best possible version of myself that I can be for today. I learned how to go within myself and face my own fears, my own darkness, and how to incorporate it with my Light, living my life in every aspect from my heart.

Please follow my adventures of a paralyzing stroke, death, rebirth, and allowance of trust in my own inner Divinity, with the realization of the very Divine we all are. Live my many failures, and how they taught me that I never failed, but learned to adapt and accept me for who I am, and eventually love me, unconditionally.

Discover with me, how I found my strength and courage to overcome the many obstacles that became triumphs, through perseverance and believing in myself. Our Awakening journey is a complex series of processes, broken down for you, as my own need for understanding of how, not why, drove me to the very extremes of my expansion beyond the 3D world.

Allow me to guide you through a different perception of navigating our interdimensional journey, with you adapting it to fit your journey, with trust and belief in your own abilities. Our journeys are unique, but the processes are still present and very manageable, without the need for self-sacrifice and needless suffering.

Join me, and my internal search for the ever-elusive authentic self, the spirit, and how I came to not only know, but to understand my Higher Self and purposes. My struggles are just as real as yours, but my perceived struggles, as I would discover, were the very blessings that have brought me to who and where I am today. A necessary and integral part of my conscious evolution, every experience brought a deeper knowing of me.

If you are truly ready to know yourself deeper than you can ever imagine, if you can allow your own dedication to your own Awakening journey, then follow my adventures with me, and get ready to meet yourself as you exist beyond the limitations you perceive. Come on… allow yourself to know freedom beyond your wildest dreams, and walk with me through trauma, pain, and victory. Life is beautiful, not easy, but magical… if you allow it to be…

Gary

Glossary

The following terms are not dictionary definitions. They are defined from an Awakening perspective meant to bring a deeper understanding as to their use on our Awakening journey.

<u>Awakening</u> means to be consciously aware of the self, existing in the moment and experiencing it without judgement, while allowing life to happen organically, living every aspect of our lives from the heart, and connecting to our own Divinity through becoming our authentic limitless selves... our spirit, while maintaining our 3D existence and existing in another dimension as our spirit selves simultaneously.

<u>Awakening BEing</u> is one who consciously chooses to live their life within the scope of an Awakening Journey. They live beyond current accepted superficial "spiritual ideals and concepts". They understand life is not about the mundane 3D desires, wants, and needs, rather, accepting with trust and allowance that life is about the spirit self and the journey inward toward the higher dimensions. They know they are defined by the spirit, not the body and its pleasures. They choose to live a heart centered existence, rising above the limitations and constructs of the accepted 3D normality.

<u>BEings</u> are sentient because they have a spirit and soul. They are sentient because they have a conscience with awareness. BEings

also include all intergalactic and higher dimensional entities, most more evolved than humans existing on this Earth, as well as our furry friends, also more advanced than us in many ways.

Collective Conscious or Stream of Consciousness is every BEing throughout the multiverse, connected by an invisible string to the Divine, therefore inseparable. We all come from the same source, therefore a part of each other, yet unique. We share a common journey while on our own personal journey, contributing to the evolution of all BEings through our personal and shared experiences. Every BEing and their journey are unique to their purposes of existence, contracted before any incarnation, and carried over from lifetime to lifetime.

Comfort zones are nice little boxes we create our entire lives, allowing us to live within familiar limitations to simplify our lives and feel safe. We live strictly within this comfort zone, believing our lives to be good and proper, and easily navigated. Unfortunately, we can neither grow nor evolve within them, and remain locked in status quo, unable to move forward. Anything outside of this and we become vulnerable, not knowing how to proceed within the discomfort of our vulnerability and without limit.

Divinity or Divine refers to what is commonly known as "God, Source etc.", which is actually pure consciousness in energy and without form. We all come from this consciousness, which is within us all. The recognition of our "inner Divinity or Divine" is awareness and acceptance of this energy within the self, and our connection is our spirit self. We all are sovereign BEings within Divinity, and unique to our journey, within the Collective Consciousness, a part of each other.

Dark Night of the Soul is a process of transformation. Its purpose is to facilitate our Awakening Journey through a phase of extreme deep emotional healing to bring us back to the spirit self and out of a 3D existence. This transformation can be quite painful as the universe forces us to face our own darkness to bring light in quantum measure. This will last as long as necessary to bring us where we need to be on our Divine path that has been neglected by the 3D self. When this process has been completed, our perceptions are aligned with our spirit self, seeing a higher truth, and our existence becomes higher dimensional.

Higher Dimensional is an existence within the self beyond the mundane 3D life, not a location in the cosmos with form. It expresses evolution beyond what we currently know and accept, where the spirit self is found. It transcends the ego-driven life with acceptance and trust, facilitating a heart-based existence through unconditional love and recognition of our Inner Divinity. It is living life as our authentic limitless self from the heart in every aspect of our life. The only way to the Higher Dimensions is through true authenticity, existing as the spirit self.

Mindset is a choice to live beyond our current truth to bring change out of our comfort zone with awareness and recognition of a need to evolve out of status quo. A change in mindset is moving above our current thought process, destroying old patterns and beliefs to be replaced by those of an Awakening existence to allow evolution. Changing our mindset is allowing ourselves to be authentic, transcending our current self-imposed limitations, bringing evolution in profound measure. This change enables us to see more possibilities, unlocking untapped potential to rise above a current state of existence.

Spirituality is a means of living above the accepted 3D self and is of the spirit, not the material world. In actuality, it is living a life as our authentic limitless self in a heart-based existence, moving away from the limitations and constructs of the 3D, inward toward the Higher Dimensions. It's knowing life is not about our physical 3D wants and desires, rather acceptance of our Inner Divinity and allowing our spirit self to guide us beyond an ego-based reality.

Vulnerability is that incredibly uncomfortable feeling as we step outside of our comfort zone, where we are raw and open to the unknown. It's allowing ourselves to expand and evolve with trust, while letting go of the illusion that we control life. Being vulnerable, we accept change, not knowing direction or what is next. It's learning to trust and believe in ourselves, and our journey to authenticity, allowing life to be as it's meant to be, not how we believe it should be. It is the only state of BEing we can learn, grow, and heal within as we break the illusions we have created through perceptions guided by the ego.

Chapter 1

Awakening

Much like you, I was tired of my life and its limitations and, quite frankly, frustrated by the lack of the life I wanted. I lived in survival mode and quite often found myself a victim to pretty much everything. I was wandering through life longing for happiness and not understanding I could change all of that. Tragedy struck, and the Universe empowered me to take the journey within to find that I already possessed all I needed. So do you. Your Awakening Journey awaits within.

Awakening cannot possibly be totally defined by words as it is a deeper understanding into truth than most can comprehend. We have the ability to exist within multiple dimensions at the same time, in as much balance as possible. How can we exist in multiple dimensions? Simply put, we are a spirit from a Higher Dimension that resides within a form present in the third dimension, existing simultaneously.

A popular saying in the spiritual community is, "We are a spirit having a human experience" and there is truth to this. We arrived from somewhere within the multiverse and chose to incarnate at this time on this planet for many reasons. No, human BEings are not the only intelligent species in the multiverse.

One reason why healing is much faster here—although harder than on most planets—is due to the atmosphere being denser. Many came here to heal their past lives while healing the current experiences of this life. Most expected to come here to speed up their evolution and instead found difficulty they could not foresee.

Many crash landed due to the heavy atmosphere and their spirits became contorted and damaged, bringing obvious challenges from the start. Many also knew before they were born that they would come here unwanted and unloved by their birth parents, which causes major trauma that can possibly last many lifetimes.

Some came here to assist Mother Earth and all of humanity with the ascension process, bringing Higher Dimensional knowledge to share with others. Others came to have various experiences to add to the Collective Conscious, as well as their own need for understanding and the experience of life elsewhere, while learning the lessons they needed. Now, we're all here, going about our business, receiving the experiences meant to help us evolve and learn. So, what is "Awakening"?

As stated earlier, it cannot be fully defined with words but this is a working definition to help with some understanding. Awakening means to be consciously aware of the self, existing in the moment and experiencing it without judgement, while allowing life to happen organically. It means living every aspect of our lives from the heart and connecting to our own Divinity through becoming our authentic, limitless selves: Our spirit. It goes much deeper than all of this and I will try to help you understand and become an Awakening BEing. You will maintain your 3D existence while existing in another dimension as your spirit self.

When we become aware of our Awakening, it may seem as though our life has been turned upside down. We suddenly feel as if we don't belong anywhere. There may be a feeling as if everything we know is somehow wrong. You would be right with these feelings because your truth has evolved as you have and that realization will impact every aspect of your life. The old you—the 3D self— is slowly being replaced by your spirit, the authentic self.

How do we deal with all this change in our lives when we have plans for our future? A good start would be to allow life to flow to you with ease. We have been taught as children that we must be in control of our lives and that is not how this actually works. "But I have to be in control, or nothing will happen as I have planned!" We must change our perception from what we were taught to how life truly is. In order to evolve we must rise above all we have been taught and believe.

We may feel lied to by every institution we have been taught to trust—including our parents—but that is not the truth. We were raised to fit into a time that no longer exists. The saying, "If it was good enough for my parents, it's good enough for me" is really not a good model for evolution. Times change, as we do, and we must keep up with the constant change of inner and outer environments. Learn to accept change, as it is the only constant in your Awakening life. Other important measures we can take to begin our evolution, besides letting go of control, are to let go of the attachments we have made to how we believe our life should be and letting go of expectations.

Having attachments gives us ownership. We believe," It is mine," our possession, or feeling owned by another, an object, or idea. We will have many attachments to many things, most of which are material, but we can also have attachments to emotions. One of the worst attachments we have are to people—mainly partners and children—or perhaps even an infatuation. We own nothing in this life except that which is of our person; our emotions, actions, reactions, thoughts, responses, and words. Non-attachment is knowing that no one and no thing has ownership of us.

When we have no expectation, we cannot be disappointed. An expectation is a projected outcome designed for our own personal gain. This takes us out of living in the moment and has us living in the future, which is an illusion and does not exist. It also does not allow life to happen—or to come to us organically—because we already have our desired outcome and are disappointed when it is not what we wanted.

We must remember that we wrote our story before we came here, so life is not about how we think it should be or what we want. We will always have free will and choice, but ultimately we will be brought the experiences necessary for that particular time. What matters is how we respond or react, as it sets in motion all that is to follow. It is always better to respond than react.

All too often, we will find ourselves in a most uncomfortable situation and we just need to leave because something feels incredibly off. This could be your spirit sending a warning you need to heed. Your own energy will respond to any given situation and you should listen to your intuition.

When you feel comfortable again and have free time, relive the experience and see if you can pinpoint the root cause of what triggered your inner alarm system. That way when you have a similar experience you will have a reference point. See if there are similarities and keep a mental log. This is also you learning to trust yourself and honing your intuition.

The Awakening Process has to be destructive because we are tearing down all that we were, becoming our authentic self, our spirit. Everything we thought we knew—who we were told to be, how to act, all the projections put on us as children—is not who we truly are. This is a process of rediscovering ourselves, going within, and finding the authentic self. Everything before our awareness of Awakening needs to be undone.

So, how do we take all those years from our lives and just change them? The only change we can bring is to the self. By being consciously aware, we begin to examine ourselves, our nuances, perceptions, triggers, thoughts, choices—the list is incredibly long. We must go within and get to know our true self, not who we've been told to be. Awakening is, in part, unbecoming who we were taught to be.

Some of us will discover hidden or latent gifts and abilities that have always been a part of us. As we become more aware of our self, there will come a trust we never had before, and a belief in our self we could never find. We begin to understand why certain things bother us, why we are drawn to specific places or things, and why we are afraid to even try some things.

Memories we have forgotten will pop up from situations or experiences and we will feel emotions we had chosen to stuff down and forget about. As they come back—and they will—they will need to be healed. At some point on our journey, we all will need to embrace the vulnerability of the internal struggle and allow our evolution to happen organically.

You will feel as if your very world has been destroyed, and indeed, that is part of the process. You are okay and you're going to be okay. You are always exactly where you are meant to be on your journey and you will experience exactly what you need to learn, grow, and heal as you evolve. You will feel every emotion there is and find a new depth to what you feel, perhaps with an intensity you could never imagine before.

You will be in awe and fear at the same time, and like the sea and land, will face peaks and valleys—riding a wave of ebb and flow with a frightening uncertainty at times. This is where we need to learn to trust ourselves, our journey, the process, and God. When we can put all this together, we can begin the process of surrender.

I can't stress enough the importance of trust on your Awakening Journey, especially in yourself. You are, in essence, not only meeting yourself on a different level in a new way, you're saying goodbye to who you thought you were and saying hello to your true self. The adventure you're going on is amazing, painful, beautiful, traumatic, inspiring, and scary all at the same time.

I remember how my awareness began as a young teen, going through puberty and an Awakening at the same time. It was the most horrific time of my life and I would absolutely go through it again to have the beautiful life I have now. My experiences would bring me to my present state of being with a whole new understanding of myself and life.

You may feel that you are learning so very much as it all seems new, but in truth, you're remembering what you had forgotten. For some reason—unbeknownst to me and many others—we have amnesia when we come into this existence and we spend the rest of our life trying to remember what we have forgotten from all of our past lives!

Locked deep within you is all you need on your journey and you will find it all as you discover yourself, allowing the natural transformation to happen. Don't fight what is happening. Once it has begun, there is no stopping it, so please keep it as simple as possible. If you fight this evolution, there will be needless suffering, born from non-acceptance of what is meant to be.

When we resist our organic evolution, the Universe has to step in. It may become ugly, messy, and even more painful than it already is, but we always have a choice. You can allow it to come and embrace your evolution, or fight a battle you can't win. I speak from experience here as I first denied my own evolution, ending up going through a very traumatic Dark Night of the Soul, as many of us do.

Because I had no understanding, I allowed my fears to take over my life and came within minutes of suicide, all because I could not face my own darkness. It wasn't cowardly, I just couldn't trust and believe in myself to know I had the strength and courage to overcome every pain and trauma I had experienced.

My life became dark and negative. I went into the rabbit hole so deep that I couldn't see a way out. I was mean and pushed good people away. I lost the ability to see any kindness or beauty and honestly believed the only way out was to end my life. I truly hated myself and my life and often sat crying like a child, unable to see any light.

In 1999, I was listening to what I believed to be the last song of my life with the gun in my mouth. I truly listened to the words of the song "Learning to Live" by Dream Theater. For the first time in way too long, I thought about someone other than myself: My family. My brother and grandfather had just crossed over and I was overcome with sudden guilt as I saw the pain on their faces, imagining them viewing my body in the casket.

In that moment of guilt, I laid the gun down, shaking and crying uncontrollably. I heard a voice for the second time in my life—it said that it was not yet my time. The first time I had heard this same voice was five years earlier during a stroke in which I was brain dead for approximately 10 minutes, waiting in the darkness for what seemed an eternity.

That voice—that realization of my own accountability of how my action would affect others—is what stopped me from blowing out the back of my head. I still hear that voice speaking to me. It enables me to put into words what I remember, and share it with you in hopes that it can make a difference in your life.

I have been to the very bottom with nothing to lose and nowhere to go. As I look back on it now, I see a blessing so immense, I still cannot fathom the impact on my life. You see, if we have nothing to lose and nowhere to go, we have everything to gain and everywhere to go, depending on our perception. I knew at that moment that I had broken through my own darkness and into my own Light, but it took the most intense emotions I could possibly feel for me to realize all of this.

I began a healing journey and my Awakening went into overdrive. Here I am today, with everything I need. I love myself and I have the ability to help others on their journey, as well as help them heal emotionally. I can finally say, "I Love my life!" ... truly. What a blessing to lose one's self in darkness to find they are the very Light they seek.

I have been to the edge of sanity, looked into the pits of my own hell, and conquered much of what used to conquer me every day. I will heal emotionally until it is time for me to return to the spirit world and beyond. I will continue to do all I can to allow my evolution to be what it is meant to be. I was learning the importance of trust.

I tell you my story because I would like you to know that regardless of what we have been through, there is always something to hold onto, some kind of hope that will carry us through the deepest darkness of our inner self. We can overcome anything we experience. We can heal the traumas and pains of our emotional body and our physical body as well.

See, my story started long before this incident of wanting to end my life. I recovered from a stroke that left me paralyzed on my left side. I lost the ability to speak and my frontal lobe was completely destroyed as I was brain dead for about 10 minutes. My personal struggles became a fight for the very life I would think about ending down the road.

28 years later, no one can even see that I overcame that event. I don't limp, don't have a slur, or problem with speech. I have some neurological issues that aren't evident and I also healed my physical body—we will get to that in a different chapter. The way I see it, if I can do all of this, then anyone can.

It takes a mindset—a change in perception and trust and belief in yourself—with dedication and determination to want it bad enough to make it happen. I proved the doctors wrong when I was given my last rites and told I would probably die. They didn't know that. It was my life and I wasn't willing to allow myself to die just yet.

I have seen death twice and have come back to continue my journey in a most spectacular way. Now I share what I have learned with you. How I did this will not work for everyone, but you can adapt my methods to suit your journey. I pray that when you have finished reading my story of evolution, you'll find your truth, not mine.

I pray that even if I help just one of you reading this book, I have fulfilled my Divine Purpose of bringing change to this world. When I am finally called home, I will leave knowing that I did what I came here to do and can go in peace. Some of this gets very involved with process, so please, reread parts if you need to. Thank you for taking the time to read the words of knowledge I have to share with this world and whomever can read this throughout the cosmos.

...Trust Yourself

Trust your journey

Trust the process

Trust God...

Chapter 2

Healing The Physical And Mental Self

So many of us have physical pain, trauma, and ailments that are chronic. Many of us have been given a death sentence from some kind of dis-ease and diagnosis. We just accept the prognosis, feeling we are locked into whatever the doctor says without question, and accept our own demise without a fight. I personally was told 28 years ago—a result from a massive stroke—that I would be fortunate to have death visit me.

The doctor's exact words were, "Mr. Hinebaugh, if you live for the next 72 hours, you'll never walk, talk, and someone will have to care for you the rest of your life…". I was 31 years old and as far as could be determined from MRI's and a battery of neuro-psyche exams, I was brain dead for about 10 minutes. No, I shouldn't even be alive by medical standards, yet here I was listening to this crap.

I was married then, my then-wife in the hospital room with me. I was paralyzed on my left side, I couldn't speak, and would later discover my frontal lobe had been completely destroyed from lack of oxygen. I had also suffered a brain aneurysm. I signaled to my then-wife to bring me a note pad to respond to the doctor.

I had simply written, "Fuck you" on the paper and showed it to him. He was shocked at my response and actually took offense. I was only 31 and so not ready to die. I could not accept his words of doom. It really pissed me off and I motioned him to leave and didn't want to see him. *How dare you tell me this to my face and expect me to accept it.*

I laid there thinking, *don't tell me I'm going to die or just be a beast of burden the rest of my life.* So many thoughts came rather quickly, and I just couldn't accept what he had said. I had some tough days ahead either way, or not. I rejected his implications and thought him rather arrogant for even telling me this.

To this day, I'm not sure if he truly believed his own words, or if it was meant to motivate me and bring a desire to live. Either way, I could not accept his prognosis. I told my then-wife to go home, because I really needed to sort this out in my own mind, and come to some sort of understanding with God as to my own reality, or demise.

I remember, as I laid there thinking it all through, *I'm not ready to die, and I certainly am not going to be a beast of burden to anyone. I would rather die than have to be taken care of the rest of my life because that isn't an option either.* So, what to do? Well, it was out of my hands as life had taught me already. I didn't have control of my life. My only logical option was to allow life to happen as it was meant to and accept what it had in mind for me. I just hoped it had me in mind tomorrow and I resigned myself to allow sleep to take over.

I prayed that night before I slept. I never really prayed for myself before. I begged God to take me because I was not about to live my life with the limitations the good doctor had just given me. I begged for death. I wasn't afraid of dying and never had been because I knew it was a cycle of life. I knew that I would return to my Light-Self and I would continue to exist, just not on this plane and dimension.

When I awakened from my slumber the following morning, I remember saying in my mind, "… okay…. What are we going to do today?" I looked around and knew I was still alive because it was not my time to die. I also knew, from this moment on, I couldn't overcome this on my own and asked for all the help I could get.

But what was my first step in physical and emotional healing? How was I going to heal? I had no clue, but that night before I had completely surrendered my life to the Divine and let go of all control, of any expectations and attachments I had concerning my life. I understood, somehow, that I would overcome all of this.

In the instant the stroke occurred, my life had changed, never to be the same, and I was never to be the same again. So, as I laid there, waiting for the nurse to come in so I could pee, I gave thanks for allowing me to wake up. I gave gratitude for everything I could think of, but most of all, I gave thanks for my life.

I made a promise that day to live my life, not for me, ever again. I promised that day to dedicate my life, however I could, to fulfill the Divine purpose I didn't yet know. In 28 years, that has not changed, and I still dedicate my life to the Divine purpose I now know, and every day I still surrender my life to live as I Am meant to.

Today, 28 years after the event, no one would ever know it even happened. I have no limp, no problem speaking, and my mind is quick and full of information. I still have problems with recall on occasion and I have days when my thought process just isn't there. But the point I make is that I healed not only the physical self, but the mental self as well. It can be done if you want it bad enough. Dr. Joe Dispenza wrote a book about his journey from paralysis to being mobile, so now you have two references for proving we can heal the body. It will take dedication, determination, and an amazing will and desire, but it can be done.

How do we learn to heal the physical body? Like anything else in life, there is a process that takes time, dedication, and courage, with allowing the process to work. It also begins with awareness, trust, and believing in yourself, and knowing we can indeed talk to our body. Rehabilitating the physical body was painful, arduous, and quite scary.

Doing the necessary work to once again use my paralyzed left side meant I had to learn how to walk and regain use of my left arm and hand as well. The hardest lesson for me was trusting the physical therapists with my body and allowing them to show me what they had learned from years of knowledge. I had to trust them with my life, because I knew at any moment my leg would give out and buckle, sending me crashing to the floor.

Had I fallen and bumped my head hard enough, I could have re-injured the aneurysm, resulting in probable death. I remember the anxiety in my first session because I had to trust myself and God as well. I had to learn to let go of the control I thought I had and put my faith in them, myself, the process, and God if I wanted to walk again. I was determined to do what was necessary no matter what I had to endure. They put a wheelchair in front of me, helped me stand, and gave beautiful words of encouragement, but I just stood and cried because I didn't believe in myself. I didn't trust myself.

My resolve overtook my fear and I put my full weight on my right leg and tried to pull my left leg forward. Nothing. I tried again and again. The more I tried, the more I cried. I remember at some point screaming my pain for anyone within earshot to hear. I collapsed in a heap on the floor, crying like a child, feeling failure and doubt, shame, and apprehension. They let me lay there and get it out of my system, all the raw emotions of the whole event. When I had finished feeling sorry for myself, the therapist spoke to me, asking me if I was okay. I nodded yes and he sat on the floor next to me and said, "Let's talk."

We had grown up together from grade school, not really friends, but what he said made the difference I needed to hear. He acknowledged my fear and doubt and said I had choice in all of this. I could either choose to make this happen, or I could choose to live the rest of my life in this condition. He told me how hard it would be to regain the use of my left side and said he would help me as much as he could, but ultimately, it was up to me if I wanted to walk again. *Damn.* I knew he was right in everything he said. It was up to me and although I would be helped, I was the one who had to do the hard work and endure the physical and emotional pain of rehabilitation.

I was just challenged and I never walked away from a challenge no matter how hard or stupid it was. I had to prove to myself that I could and would overcome this sudden limitation. I was in victim mode for quite a while after the event, trying to think what I had done so wrong to deserve this. As I pondered this question one day, I received a clear vocal reply, and it was not my voice.

I had heard this voice before and again felt the loving energy as it spoke. This voice told me I had done nothing to deserve this and that there was purpose to what I was going through. *Okay. What was the purpose?* The voice told me that I didn't need to know and that right now what was important was that I did all I could to overcome the resulting paralysis.

Okay. So I was on a need-to-know basis with this voice. I was to trust this voice in my head. Right. *I don't trust anyone, not even myself, so now I have to learn to walk, talk, use my left hand and arm, and retrain my brain to take over the functions that were destroyed in the stroke.* Right. *And how am I to be expected to do all that the voice is asking me to do?*

I'm just a human being, not some superhero from a comic book, and I certainly don't have superpowers to do what you want me to do. This was too much for one person to take on and it's impossible to do any of this. It's physically not humanly possible. Okay. Oh, I believe I've just been challenged again. I believe I let fly some pretty lengthy expletives at this point that would have made a sailor blush.

Wow! The voice said all this was very possible, but I had to trust and believe in myself so much that there could be no doubts as to what I was able to do. I had to put all my trust in God. I was pissed at God at this point for allowing this to happen to me and even accused God of making this happen to me. I had to blame someone because I surely didn't ask for this.

How could I ever trust and believe in a God that would allow me to endure this, and furthermore, make me endure this? I would spend hours screaming and yelling at God, saying some pretty mean and nasty things, and never received one response. Well, God certainly didn't listen to me either. I hated God. And I honestly believed God didn't like me.

I felt alone in my plight. No one could help me, and God not only allowed me to go through this, but he abandoned me as well. *I'm so screwed. How in the hell am I going to do all that has been asked of me? Why is this happening to me? I didn't deserve any of this, yet here I am having to deal with this new reality that I didn't ask for. I quit. There is no way I can do any of this, so I quit.*

Just accept that I'll never be able to heal physically, and someone will have to care for me the rest of my life. Wait. What? No. I am not going through life as either a vegetable or a beast of burden. These were not options for me and I would not allow either scenario to be my fate. Okay, so since these were not options, then the only option left was to do whatever I had to do to heal, and do everything the doctor said I would never do. Challenge taken.

This was a turning point in my life, to know I was in for the fight of—and for—my life. Failure was not an option either. Failure to me was admitting defeat, which made me a loser... again. I was tired of being a failure in everything I had ever done. I was tired of feeling sorry for myself, feeling unworthy and undeserving. Challenge taken.

It all became a challenge to me that I could not fail, and I could not lose, because I was tired of coming in last place. I was tired of being looked down upon by society and myself. Somewhere in this jumbled mess of a thought process I found my will, my resolve, my determination, and as my dad used to say, I found a pair. I could not allow any of this in my life any longer. *I will succeed at all cost.* I had to.

Hope. I finally saw hope in my despair and self-pity. My resolve was to stop playing the victim card and to somehow figure out how I was going to overcome this. I had made up my mind that this was something I absolutely could not allow myself to be defined by. I made up my mind that this was just a glitch in my life and, somehow, I was going to heal.

There was no turning back for me at this point. It was game on and I allowed my determination to take control. I dedicated every waking second of my life to making damn sure I was going to prove that lying doctor wrong. How dare he tell me I was never going to be anything other than what he said. I listened to that my whole childhood and I was done listening to it.

Oh my. Where did that come from? Now I had something to prove to someone other than myself. Those words stung, and do even now. I had to prove myself worthy of looking those other two in the eye and having the pleasure of telling them, "I have done exactly what you said I couldn't."

I was bound and determined that, one day, I would show them both how wrong they were. *In your face... I'm going to prove you wrong.* And so, I set the tone for all that would take place the rest of my life. I had purpose. I had a reason to exist. I finally felt that I was indeed someone.

Having made up my mind to heal, I went full-go with determination and drove myself to the limit every day. I didn't care how bad the pain was, I had to push through it. I had to walk again, talk again, and I had to work again. I had to become useful and I had to do it for me. I healed those shaming and hurtful words those two spoke to me, and now I was on a mission and there was no one and nothing that could stop me.

I had been on my spiritual journey for most of my life and during the New Age movement there was one bit of wisdom I took and made my daily mantra:" We reinvent who we are every day, doing something today to become the man I know myself to be." I would repeat this to myself as I broke through the physical pain every day.

So, how did I learn to overcome all of this? What did I do? Using my spiritual background, I knew that when we talk to ourselves, we change what we need to about ourselves. I started talking to the body and to the cells in my body. I started to be loving and compassionate with myself, giving myself encouragement and reward for accomplishing a short-term goal.

I was given "simple" tasks by the therapists such as pinning a clothes pin to the clothesline. I had lost eye-hand coordination from the stroke, and I had also lost depth perception, so this was hard for me to accomplish. What I took for granted in my previous life—before the stroke—was now incredibly hard for me to do.

The therapists brought me kid's toys such as placing a round or square peg in their corresponding holes. These were things I had lost the ability to do. I was now at the learning level of a two-year-old child once again, but I was 31 years old. How humiliating. But I was determined to one day be able to do everything I could before the stroke and so much more.

As I worked to regain these skills I had lost, I spoke to my body telling it how to connect to the brain, and allow the neuron receptors to fire in my brain and allow me to put that square peg in the square hole and the round peg in the round hole. When I wasn't in therapy, I would walk through my yard, trying hard to stop dragging my leg and trying to picking it up, to actually walk.

I would tell the brain to pick my leg up and move it forward. I would tell my leg to use its muscles and pick itself up and move it forward. Every movement I had to make came with instruction to the body on how to make that movement, how to connect to the brain and central nervous system.

I had to tell the body and brain the process for everything I did over and over. I had to focus my attention on telling my body and brain how to put that square peg in the square hole. I had already learned how to do all of this as a child, yet here I was once again learning how to do it with the intelligence of a grown man.

I spoke to every cell in my body, telling the muscle structure how to mend and become useful, telling it over and over every day how to make new cell structure. I told it how to make new cells to replace the damaged cells and envisioned it happening as I spoke to the body, seeing new cells taking over the old, damaged cells.

I did this with the central nervous system as well, seeing new cell growth replacing old, damaged cells and creating new nerves—forming, rerouting, connecting themselves in a new pattern, bypassing the old central nervous system that had been damaged. I did this with every breath I took because I would not settle for anything less than a total recovery.

My entire focus was on my body and brain. My will, determination, and resolve became stronger daily and I allowed myself to become transformed with all the processes I had to undertake daily. Teaching the damaged brain was the hardest therapy I would endure. I was told that it was impossible to retrain or reteach damaged areas, that all the skills I once had were gone, and that I would never heal the brain.

Don't tell me I can't do something and don't put limits on my life. I was determined to do what I had to do, because what they told me wasn't good enough for me and I would not accept what they had told me. There had to be some way within myself to undo what this glitch had done, and I was determined to do the "impossible."

The frontal lobe is the area of the brain that controls our "executive functions"—math, order, prioritization, and so many other functions we take for granted. I took it all for granted. Everything I did, all I was, me... I took it all for granted. Why shouldn't I? Well, wake up one day not able to do these things and see how long you take them for granted when they're gone.

Never in my life did I imagine that one day I would have to overcome everything I did, but the fact was, it happened. So how did I retrain my damaged brain to do what I was told was impossible? I worked hard using my brain every second I had a chance, never stopping—no matter how bad my migraine was or how many tears it caused me.

The migraines came every day and those days turned into several months. The doctors never could differentiate between cluster migraines or new ones daily, but it didn't matter. The fact was that they were severe and the worse they got, the more I cried. That only made them worse, but I had to push through as failure was not an option.

I found an old deck of cards and found an opportunity with them to retrain my brain. I played every kind of solitaire I could and I even went back to an old game I used to enhance my intuitive ability, guessing at first if the next card was higher or lower than the face up card. It does work in nurturing our natural abilities of intuition.

I played this every chance I could, no matter how bad my pain was. It was also an opportunity to regain use of my left hand and arm as an occupational therapy method. I started to try and use my left as my dominant hand instead of my right. I would force myself to pull the card with my left hand, although that was almost impossible at first.

I would go outside to the clothesline with my clothes pin and try to put it on the line every day. It was difficult for me to accept that I couldn't do it at first and became frustrated easily. So many times I would break down and cry because I was trying so hard and seeing so little progress. I'm an Aries, so not seeing forward progress was the most frustrating thing I had to face.

I had to change my thought process throughout this daily routine I had created for myself, because I would get frustrated and then angry. I realized it was just making matters worse for me. I had to stop being a victim to my limitations and allow the healing process to be what it needed to be.

I had to find patience, and as an Aries, I didn't have any. That is still a lesson I'm learning. Every time I felt frustration coming on, I would take some deep breaths, give myself love and compassion, and constantly tell myself I was okay, and I was going to be okay. I learned to calm myself when it came, so I could do what I needed to that day.

I struggled with every movement I made. I had to accept that for now—until I healed myself—this was my life. I had to accept that I was not even half the man I was, because here I was, disabled, and I was somehow less than who I truly was. *Oh poor, poor little old me.* I truly got tired of feeling sorry for myself and the pity parties I would throw every day.

I had to stop the madness I was creating, not only for me, but for my then-wife and stepchildren. It was bad enough that I had to live like this, but I did not have to project all of this onto them or anyone else. I had to be aware of myself on an incredibly deep level so I would not take everything out on them.

I don't remember when I stopped talking about what I was going through, because it was my pain, my problem, and it wasn't fair to anyone for me to force it on them. To this day I don't talk about my pain—physical or emotional. It's mine, I own it, and I'll keep it to myself. I'm not about to make someone else miserable just because I am.

Okay, perhaps I'm just a little bit selfish on this, and I'm sure my beautiful present-day wife does agree, but she has understanding and respect for this part of me. Somehow, all of this was not only changing me on a personal level, it was changing me on a spiritual level. I had to go incredibly deep within myself to find my strength, courage, and whatever else I needed to find just to live this screwed up existence. Little did I know how this part of my journey was meant to bring me to where I am today.

The daily challenges were taking a toll on me physically and mentally, and every day, I prayed for it to end, even if it meant I was to die, and some days I begged for death. My will, determination, dedication, and resolve were beat down every step of the way and I could not see an end to what I had to endure.

My faith suffered, my marriage suffered, and somewhere along the way, the people I considered a friend were nowhere to be found. I had no visitors and pretty much not even my family was there for me. I had little support. My then-wife did what she was able to do, and I will thank her until the day I die for her part in my recovery, but I was basically on my own.

I had no one to depend on but me, and when I needed help the most, I couldn't even find God in any of this. I put on my big boy panties and worked harder at healing than I ever had before, putting so much effort into anything I did. I had to. I had to walk, talk, and become a functioning member of society again.

I had purpose, I had a life—although, not much of one—and I was going to heal. I kept on playing the card games daily as the migraines would allow. Somehow, I did rewire my brain and the neuron receptors began to fire again. I slowly started to speak, formulating words at first. Knowing what you want to say and not being able to say it is very frustrating.

I never had a problem speaking my mind or knowing what I wanted to say. Somehow, the connection between my brain and mouth had been severed and I don't know how this works within the body, so I won't even attempt to explain. I couldn't read because I couldn't comprehend words and what they meant, and how a sentence flowed to bring meaning.

That was lost when the frontal lobe was destroyed. I had a wonderful personal library of over 700 books I had read and now all I could do was lament how I didn't know how to read anymore. So, back to being a two-year-old and learning to speak and read again. Did I mention my frustration? I had what appeared to be an impossible task ahead of me, but somehow I had to make it possible.

I didn't know how, but that didn't stop me from just doing it, figuring it out along the way. When I began to be able to speak again, I had an issue with recall on top of everything else. How was I supposed to put a sentence together if I couldn't pull what I wanted to say from my memory? How could I communicate my needs, what I felt, and what I was going through?

I simply couldn't, so I stopped trying. I was locked inside myself, unable to respond, unable to find what I needed within me. The old me was being completely destroyed because I had to reinvent myself in every way. As I look back on the whole experience, that stroke became the biggest stroke of luck I would ever have.

My step kids were young and had books that helped them learn to read. There was an opportunity right there for me to learn how to read and speak. This was more responsible for my recovery than anything I could try. I gathered a few of their books and hid them under my chair because I was 31 years old and ashamed of the fact that I couldn't even read a child's book as well as my step kids.

When no one else was around, I would pull one out and try to speak as I tried to read. Some of the words I couldn't pronounce—let alone remember what they meant—but I wasn't about to let that stop me from trying. I'm sure my step kids would have had a few good laughs with me and I'm certain, had I asked, would have helped me sound them out as I had helped them.

Speech came to me slowly, not only in timeframe, but physically as well. My throat would tire quickly, which only made it harder for me to speak, limiting any effectiveness my efforts could bring. I was fighting an uphill battle on every front of my being. Imagine: A college-educated 31-year-old man, unable to read a child's book.

I was overwhelmed constantly in my recovery, but I was on a mission, and I wouldn't rest until I had made a full recovery. I kept pushing through the pain, frustration, anger, doubt, and shame I felt every moment along the way. The harder I tried, the more I went through. I don't recall when, but at some point, I gave up trying. I just didn't care anymore.

It had become more than I could handle, trying so hard every day to overcome this impossibility of recovery. I had more coming at me than what I have mentioned that made progress seem improbable. On top of all I had already faced, I began having seizures that would basically erase my efforts and send me backwards in my progress.

Mine were called absence seizures, which are not at all like grand mal or petite mal seizures. They would devastate me for weeks, trying just to recover from them. At first, they scared me terribly because I thought I was having more strokes, as I had no understanding of them or what caused them. They lasted almost 20 years before they somehow ended.

The seizures were debilitating. My skin would turn grey, breathing went to barely existing, my pulse dropped to around 30 beats per minute, and my mental faculties would all but disappear. Those around me would ask me questions and I would respond 10-20 minutes later. It was a total neurological disconnect, and I was closer to death with each seizure.

Those who witnessed them were scared I wouldn't survive, as was I. Some would last up to an hour, some I barely noticed while others did. It would take me weeks to recover from one, and sometimes I would sleep for days. All progress I had made was lost from one seizure to the next, complicating the healing process.

I never gave up. How could I? This was my new reality and I had to trust on a level I believed impossible, but I was the only one who could heal me. Or was I? The blame game with God had faded with acceptance of my reality. I kept going back to the day the stroke occurred, remembering that I couldn't do this alone. My trust in God went into overdrive with unconditional love.

Somehow, I found a way to trust and believe in myself. I had no other choice. Live or die, I had to succeed on my mission of complete healing, and again, failure was not an option. My determination and dedication to heal the physical and emotional self consumed every aspect of my existence. There was no other way for me. Not then, not ever again. Life had to continue regardless of my state of being.

I write this, 28 years later, with tears of remembrance of the pains and trauma I lived through. How did I truly endure all of this? The only way I can think of is that I was not meant to live as the doctor had told me. This whole process was a part of my Awakening Journey. I had contracted for this before I came here, and cannot imagine what I was drinking when I signed the contract.

Through this incredible journey of healing, I learned acceptance, allowance, trust, patience, and that I was indeed more than I had given myself credit for. I learned how to navigate the rest of my life through any kind of trauma or pain. Most of all, I learned to be compassionate with myself.

I learned what grace means and that hope cannot be lost. Ever. A BEing without hope has nothing to lose, but how we choose to address that sets the rest of our life in motion, or our demise. My brother—who would succumb to cancer several years after my stroke—had a saying that got us both through some very hard times.

He would smile when anyone would say that something was impossible, responding with this life lesson:" The only thing that's impossible is to stretch a gnat's ass across a washboard..." Once we have made up our minds and we dedicate ourselves to that mindset, we become an unstoppable force.

In the words of basketball coaching legend Jim Valvano in a speech on March 4, 1993, while living with cancer: "Don't give up, don't ever give up..." I remember his words spoken that day, and the impact it had on my life and the healing process I was going through at the time. Those words gave me the ability to carry on during the days when I felt lost and sorry for myself.

Chapter 3

Trust

Trusting ourselves is one of the most important personal traits we can possess on our Awakening Journey. I can't stress enough how important this is on your journey. Implicit trust of the self is knowing you can do just about anything that is physically, mentally, and spiritually possible. You are, after all, a limitless BEing capable of so much more than you believe.

We have lifetimes of wisdom within ourselves and knowledge from our ancestors that gives us many clear reference points to draw on, but we must trust this knowledge. Any time we are uncertain what our next response or reaction should be, trust that your spirit knows what is needed. *Trust.*

Trust goes hand in hand with believing in ourselves. Unfortunately, since birth we are often told "...you can't do that..." Those are not our limitations, but theirs, and they are projecting that belief onto you. There are many areas we don't have an ability to succeed in, as we feel we need to or want to, so we should have no expectations on ourselves as to outcome.

You can, however, believe in yourself enough to try your best regardless of outcome, and at least you will have tried your best. It is no failure to not have the ability, it is just that you are unable at this time to find success. When we say," I have failed" we have put an end to that experience and there is no possible outcome we can find satisfactory.

Edison was asked, " Isn't it a shame that with the tremendous amount of work you have done you haven't been able to get results?" Edison replied, "Results! Why man, I have gotten lots of results! I know several thousand things that won't work!" His perception was not one of failure, but of success in finding what doesn't work.

He could have been hard on himself, called himself a failure, and felt shame. Instead, he took it in stride without judgement and allowed the experiment to be what it truly was. It was not his failure, but what didn't work for that one experiment. Edison had the ability to change his perception to realistically allow truth and not self-defeating judgement.

We cannot base any further similar experiences on a single prior experience, as the variables are different and not related to the past experience. Our need to compare the present to the past is a major error on our behalf and there is a need to change that old pattern. This is the old adage of comparing apples and oranges at its finest. Every experience is fresh and new, and when we have no judgement, we realize the truth within it, and we can see it and grow from it.

There are four points I make to all of my clients: Trust yourself, trust your journey, trust the process, and trust God. Let's talk about trusting your journey. I had stated earlier that we signed contracts before our arrival in this form. Certain events will take place in our lives with other spirits. Our free will gives us opportunities to change the course of our journey many times in our existence, but ultimately, we are always where we are meant to be on our journey.

Our journey will always have peaks and valleys, meaning, ups and downs. We have to learn to take the good with the bad, adapting to every conceivable situation with ease. We must allow life to happen and come to us in order to experience what is necessary. When we try to control life, we will miss out on some very important experiences, missing opportunities to learn, heal, and grow. It is imperative we let go of control in all aspects of our lives. We will not evolve if we try to control what life brings.

Trying to understand everything in our lives is not only futile, but totally unnecessary. We did not come here to know why everything happens or even to understand it. This is, again, controlling. Many times, what we experience will not have the meaning we attach to it, and we miss out on what we were actually meant to learn.

This happens when we judge our experience, and try to see from our own perspective, which many times is not actually what took place. Be aware of your thoughts and emotions, and you'll catch yourself controlling many aspects of yourself and your life. Trust your journey and allow life to happen organically.

Our journey will come with experiences that are incredibly painful. We may feel a desire to leave this life because the experience is far too traumatic to bear. We are never given more than we can handle, and many times, we will again need to change our perspective. A common 3D response when trauma exists is to place the blame on God or another for allowing this to come into our lives.

The hard truth is God did not do this to you. For some reason that we may never know, it was an experience placed on our journey by us before we came into existence. At this time, we need to remember there are reasons for everything that happens, most we don't need to know.

A lesson we all need to learn is that instead of asking, *why is this happening to me*, playing the victim role, we can ask, *where can I learn, heal, and grow from this?* Stepping out of the victim role and being able to experience without judgement changes the energy of the experience. I have had many events where I was traumatized, and learned at a later time the experience wasn't about me nor meant for me, but I was affected just the same.

It is hard for us to understand that just because something happens to us, doesn't mean it was about us, or meant for us. We are often players in an experience meant for someone else, but remembering we contracted with other spirits before we came here for specific events to take place. Our ego will be the first voice to whine and complain about anything that disagrees with its perception.

All too often we will have a series of events leaving us traumatized and feeling quite bad about our lives, not being able see out of the hole we feel we have been buried in. We lose the ability to see the good in life, the beauty, and we only end up manifesting bad things in our lives.

Again, we need to change our perspective and motivate ourselves to see the good and the beautiful once again. Please remember that everything we go through is temporary and there is another side with a better version of ourselves. This is why trust is an absolute must on our Awakening Journey. Without trust, there will be no evolution.

It's easy for us, while in the 3D, to lose our perspective when we feel as if our world is spinning out of control and crashing down around us. This is, again, a victim mentality and survival mode. Remembering that everything happens for a reason, ask, *what is there for me to learn from this*, and not *why is this happening.*

Start asking yourself questions. *What are my triggers? What am I missing through this? What can I do to help myself? What needs healed from this?* When we go within and ask ourselves questions, we have understanding of some very important logistics about ourselves. Now we begin to see an important part of our journey through our recognition that we are indeed learning and practicing self-mastery.

This is how layered our journey is, and through awareness, we find recognition of a whole new perspective on our journey, not just about us, but our life and how we truly sabotage so many aspects of our journey. Unfortunately, no one taught us this as we were growing up, so we have no reference point or understanding of what we really should be doing in life. Breaking down our walls, busting the projections forced upon us, and changing old patterns and beliefs will become a way of life, if you are dedicated and persistent in your efforts to evolve.

How can we trust the process if we don't know what the process is? The process is you shifting from your old 3D self to your authentic and limitless self, your evolution from forced projections and who you were made to be as a child. It is a stripping away of the old energies and perceptions to freedom and self-mastery.

The process is going deep within the self to face our darkest fears, overcoming them, and healing the traumas of perhaps many lifetimes, doing the emotional healing needed to evolve. The process is about you, and your dedication to achieving what you were told was impossible, and learning the value of trust.

Our journey is learning to overcome what we were taught by unhealed people we trusted, meant for a time that does not exist anymore. As we evolve, so does society, and this calls for new measures of what is now considered acceptable and not acceptable criteria for a balanced life. We can no longer abide by a broken system of society, let alone live successfully within the parameters that broken society deems a "normal existence."

Rising above old beliefs and patterns, healing ancestral lines, living in harmony with the earth, and living our lives from the heart in every aspect is the paradigm shift we must implement, if mankind and earth are to survive what our ancestors have made for us. Allowing ourselves to come out of survival mode and victim mentality are opportunities for expansion and success.

All we can do is to make the changes necessary within ourselves, for we alone cannot change the world. This is a process within our Awakening, in brief, for there are many layers to many subprocesses, taking place simultaneously, bringing change. Knowing we can trust, and have trust, will take us far on our journey.

Now we explore the hardest part of trusting: Putting our trust in God. So many times in our lives we have blamed God for all that has happened in our lives that didn't correspond to our perception of an outcome to experiences. We couldn't understand our own responsibility, so we needed a scapegoat. Who else could we blame?

Certainly, we did nothing wrong, and as we have come to believe, just blame God. Okay, so at this point there is the ageless question of, "Who is God?" That will depend on you and your perception. Religion would have us believe He is an old man with a long white beard, sitting in a huge throne, looking down upon us in judgement of all we do.

Spirituality and science know God as consciousness, an energy. Some refer to this consciousness as "the Source of all that is." This is about as close to how I see Him as well. Ask yourself this please, and really spend some time with it: *How much do I trust God?* When you have spent time with this, ask yourself, *Can I even trust God?*

If we all come from the same source, The Collective Consciousness, then inside us we are all God, this conscious energy. We are all a part of each other, so therefore we all have God within us, which we will refer to as "our own inner Divinity" or "Divine." So, if we can't truly trust God, then we can't trust ourselves either.

As we evolve, we come to an understanding of the greater good, and know there is a plan in place where we all have a part to play, as millions of actions happen in synchronicity to achieve some masterful outcome. We must be able to trust that this plan is for the greater good and that our role is very specific in nature. So, indeed, we must trust ourselves, our journey, the process, and God.

When we can put all of this trust together, we have the ability to let go of the control we think we have and allow life to happen without judgement. We surrender our lives every day to the very trust we feel we cannot give, and suddenly, we realize all those years we felt we had to control every aspect of our lives, we could have trusted and just maybe our lives would have been different somehow.

Don't believe that thought for even one second. Every experience, thought, action, and reaction have made us who we are today, and it was done at precisely the right moment for us on our journey and our evolution. Please, always remember, everything happens for a reason, even though we may not see reason at the time of our experience.

How many times have we trusted another only to find disaster, betrayal, and bitterness in the end? For many of us, more than we care to admit. Trust is such an integral part of our Awakening Journey, so why did we get burned so badly at times? As empathic BEings we want to be able to trust everyone, just as we want to help everyone, when in reality, we can't. It's just not possible or plausible.

We faced the outcome of trust because it was given without discernment. We did it blindly without thought to any outcome. We allowed ourselves, at times, to be drawn into a fantasy we devised for success, or a fantasy of our perception about the individual we trusted. Learning to trust our inner Divinity, our instinct, will save us much unnecessary trauma and pain.

It truly takes much courage to trust, and strength to allow that trust to build. How many times have we lent our trust only to be blindsided and possibly hurt in a major way? That loss of trust will take a very long time to regain, if at all possible. Sometimes the damage done will be enough that we let go of the one who betrayed us and that's okay. Let them go. We must use discernment in deciding who and what to trust. Never give away trust and respect to those who are not capable of carrying that responsibility we have given them.

Our trust is as sacred as our energy, and we must use discernment in great measure to protect our innermost sanctum. Listen to your spirit, as that instinct is there as a built-in defense mechanism. We must listen to and heed that warning sent to us in many different fashions, and we need to have a deep awareness of this instinct.

We, as limitless BEings, must rely on all of our senses, especially when it comes to giving our trust to others. How does your energy respond to someone else? What is your first impression of someone? What do you see when you look into their eyes to their spirit? Give them time to show you who they truly are, not some fantasy we create for them to be.

Always go with your first impression of someone, but be willing to allow another chance. Perhaps they were having a bad day and their energy was off, their mind was elsewhere to an important event in their life. Once that second encounter is happening, really look deep as you read them, and listen to what your spirit is saying, and follow that intuition. If a single red flag pops up, then we must heed that warning. They can still be a good person and not be trusted for various reasons.

Don't give them your most sacred self, especially on a whim, without first consulting your spirit self. Always allow someone the time to show you who they truly are. We can give a small amount of trust while we allow them to show their true self. I speak mainly of the narcissist, the manipulator, and the control freak. After they feel a sense of comfort with us, they will always let their guard down and their true essence will come forward. The narcissist is usually the hardest to detect as they are on their best behavior, waiting for the right time to draw you into their trap of treachery and deceit.

There are just as many male and female narcissists in this world, willing to take us for a ride through their world. Some will take a very short time before their true nature is exposed, while others will take months or years before they initiate their plan of use. It is always good to withhold giving ourselves to them, but we must give them the opportunity to show us who they are. Again, hold that trust in reserve until you are confident, with time always on your side.

The manipulator is often just as cunning as the narcissist, but not necessarily as calculating. They have almost the same process, but instead of being drawn into a cruel game of deceit, their ways are not as subtle in most cases. Many manipulators are narcissists, so again, allow them the opportunity to show you who they are. Their modus operandi will be to extort from you whatever they want, whether it is your possession, your time, or your essence.

Either way, they will take from you all they can in an effort to gain anything they want. All too often they will deceive themselves into believing there is nothing wrong with their actions and feel quite welcome to do as they choose, without regard for what happens to their victims. We are simply a "mark," an intended victim of prey, to be used at their discretion. They will turn what you say back onto you as they have no sense of accountability, believing they can do no wrong. Their lies will always catch up to them as many are pathological liars, and they have trouble remembering all of their lies. They are bullies and wounded children who must have their way at your cost.

The control freak is always the easiest to identify of these three personalities. Their need to control every aspect of their lives—and yours—will come out almost immediately because they really aren't aware they're doing it. It has become a way of life and who they are, so there is no recognition or awareness. They have built their lives with precise measure and will have no problem projecting this onto you.

Regardless of their personality type, we must learn to set healthy boundaries to protect ourselves. Boundaries are put into place to let others know it is not okay for them to treat us poorly and without respect. We all need to speak our truth when threatened by the missteps of others. We all deserve to be treated in proper fashion with the respect we deserve. Self-love and self-respect go hand in hand, and that includes how we allow others to treat us, as well as how we treat ourselves.

Learning discernment is another vital tool in our arsenal of protecting ourselves from others, as well as our own wounded ego. Every measure we put into place for ourselves must be in place for others. This is, again, self-love and respect. Trust yourself enough to know that what your spirit is telling you is for your highest good and should never be ignored.

My wife Neha and I were having a video session with an Awakening BEing who was having trouble with understanding how to trust herself. We spoke for the entire session about certain events in her life and why the outcome was as it was. It brought a deeper understanding of how she allowed her lack of self-trust to sabotage her journey.

As we wrapped up the session, I simply said to remember we are not defined by the 3D body, but by the spirit. It dawned on her rather quickly that this is how we begin to trust ourselves, as our spirit self. The 3D self should not be left in charge, as it is led, normally, by the wounded ego.

This is the process of self-mastery working on a deeper level within our existence. When we have the awareness that we are a spirit having a human experience and not a human having a spiritual experience, we see with a much different perspective from a Higher Dimensional sense. This change in perception will bring much needed change without much effort, affecting many aspects of our lives. The spiritual journey is a journey of the spirit world, not the material world.

Those of us on Awakening Journeys have this understanding, but many fall into spiritual mythology traps through social media that is meant to distract us from our purpose. Can we trust what we read on social media? For the most part, no, because it brings into play too much concern for materialistic gain, which is not our purpose here. The spiritual journey is within—toward the spirit and away from the material world.

Many fall into spiritual ego traps without the realization that the ego is still in charge. I will suggest at this point to not take what you see on social media as truth, as most is far from truth in reality. There are some respected spiritual leaders who have withstood the test of time that we can rely upon to bring us truth. Always question what you read. There is an old saying: "It must be true if it's on the internet." I love sarcasm.

There are many ways to safeguard ourselves, and I have given you just a few to bring awareness to not allowing yourself to trust just anyone or anything. It all begins with awareness, setting healthy guidelines, and using strict discernment. Not everything is as it appears to be, and we must be able to sense when what is presented is other than truth. Always protect your most coveted assets and always trust your spirit to guide you.

Our ability, or inability, to trust is crucial to our Awakening Journey. Without trust there will be no evolution, which is part of the foundation our journey is built upon. Learning to trust takes time and patience as we are breaking old patterns and beliefs that have held us down far too long.

With our ability to trust ourselves, our journey, the process, and God, we can begin to surrender, and our Awakening Journey can be as it is meant to be, not what or how we believe it should be. Surrendering to the Divine will facilitate assurance of our evolution. We stop fighting ourselves and a natural progression, bringing an end to needless suffering and inner turmoil.

Trusting and believing in ourselves brings inner peace and a knowing that we are capable of unlocking our untapped potential. Trust allows us to know we can and must take that one extra step on our journey toward authenticity. It actually takes less energy to allow what is meant to be than trying to control our very existence.

We simply take the energy that is bound by believing we are in control, and allow our journey to be organic, freeing that energy to do what we need to do. I personally spent too much time believing I was in charge, fighting a battle that only existed in my head. This is how we sabotage our journey and all that we truly are.

Trust allows us to see truth as it is, not how we perceive it to be. It takes us out of our ego-based existence and into a heart centered one. It brings an ability stop judging ourselves, every experience, and others, in many aspects of our lives, simplifying our existence. Always trust your intuition as it never guides you away from your highest good. Your ego does though.

Chapter 4

Changing Our Mindset

We will constantly reflect on our lives as memories come back, and may feel haunted by them because they won't leave us alone. They don't come back to bother us, they come back to us to be healed. We need to allow their existence in order for them to be healed. Our journey is an upward spiral, the same as our Galaxy through space.

Every time a memory comes to us, we are obligated to pay attention to it, visit with it, find what needs to be healed, and allow ourselves to heal it. It is a never-ending cycle through which we go within ourselves, honing our skill of self-mastery, truly knowing ourselves on an even deeper level than before. This is a must on our Awakening Journey.

Once we give ourselves any type of mindset, this is what we are manifesting and what our life becomes. The moment we say we can't, we have limited ourselves and set up a block, unable to achieve what we must do. Saying we can't means we don't trust and believe in ourselves enough to carry out our current purpose on our journey.

We will be stuck there until we can step above that perception and allow ourselves the chance to be successful. We are the ones who set our own limitations. We always have choice, even within the limits and constructs of society. The choices we have are indeed our free will, with the ability to change our lives in profound measure.

The moment we make the conscious decision to change our mindset, we begin the process of becoming our authentic limitless self, and there is forward progress in our evolution. One of the hardest processes we will undertake is retraining our ego from 3D thought to that of the Higher Dimensions.

The ego is very necessary to us, and an amazing ally when we have healed and balanced it. It is vital to first understand what the ego is. It is a part of our personality—our core BEing—that has been developed from our perception of experiences and is usually a controlling part of us.

Often our reactions to an adverse situation come from our ego, and being quick to judge gets us into trouble. It is quick to respond from a place of fear that we are being controlled, and it being of a controlling nature, it will try and turn the tables, so to speak, to its advantage and take that control back. So how do we change our ego from a controlling aspect to being useful and to our advantage? It is the same process as changing old beliefs and patterns. First, there has to be awareness of the ego and then the realization that it has spoken.

It is that voice we often hear telling us what to do, how to react, and how intense our response and subsequent emotion will be.

Anger will come out from our ego as a first response. We should allow that anger to exist without allowing it to control us, even though it is part of our nature. We start looking within ourselves, searching for reasons why the trigger response was anger.

Something triggered that response and we need to figure out why it made us emotional. Allowing the emotion to exist gives us an opportunity to go back through many experiences that brought that response from our past. This is a process and may take some time, so we need to be patient and compassionate with ourselves through the healing process.

There are ways to calm our anger to lessen the emotion, but we need to honor everything we feel, know it is real, and not deny its existence. It is necessary to know that all we feel is valid, so we must accept that it is truly there and not something we have made up. Try to center your energy on your Christ Conscious Center, located just below your breast plate. This is a vital energy center that we need to have awareness of and must learn to master.

This is roughly the center of our body and carries our Divine Energy. It is a part of all of us, connecting us all. This is the third energy, the first two being masculine and feminine. If we focus on this area and our breathing at the same time will bring a calming effect, slowing our heart rate and allowing us to feel more peaceful.

Now, we can again maintain the ability to look within and see if we can trace back to the root cause of why we had that particular reaction. As we go back we will find many trigger points to be healed. As I stated earlier, this is a process and does take time and awareness. This is the healing process, as well as the process of self-mastery, and necessary to our evolution.

We must be diligent in our efforts to heal and evolve. Many spiritualists believe we need to take "me" out of the equation of our lives and allow the Oneness to exist, claiming "me" to be the ego. In reality, one of our major purposes is bettering the self — me, I, the ego—as we are also on a singular journey, doing our part to heal the Oneness and ourselves.

We can only change ourselves in our contribution to that universal healing. This is why the balanced and healed ego will be an important asset on our journey. It all starts with the awareness mentioned earlier, leading to recognition and the desire to allow change.

In essence, changing our perception of the ego will bring the change in old patterns and beliefs about ourselves, allowing the necessary healing and evolution. Hopefully, as you are reading this, you are starting to see how new patterns of awareness bring newness to our lives and the ability to change damaging patterns and beliefs.

This new understanding is the paradigm shift brought by the Awakening Process. It is never enough to suppress emotions, pushing them down, forgetting about them, believing we have let them go. These are old patterns projected onto us from an early age, often feeding our ego because we have not healed the emotional trauma.

Any time we have an adverse reaction brought by an old pattern or belief, we allow the ego to be negative and controlling. Changing our perspective from not healing our emotions, as they surface, to that of needing to heal them immediately is, in part, retraining our ego. Awareness of the egoic response will enable us to make the necessary changes.

All this may seem confusing at first, which would be normal. Any time we are in the process of bringing something new into our world, our ego and mind will remind us time and again this is not what we know, creating an inner conflict that is uncomfortable. Within this vulnerability of uncertainty is where we are growing and learning. Embrace this vulnerable state.

Diligence in our efforts to retrain the ego and the mind will bring the wanted results in tearing down the old to bring the new. Any time something new is introduced, there is struggle. This doesn't mean we are failing—we are instead succeeding. The old has to be destroyed in order for the new to exist. As the old is being destroyed we experience chaos. Out of that chaos comes order, starting slowly, and building momentum with time.

We are coming out of the darkness—which was our 3D existence—into the light of our evolution and into a Higher Dimension, bringing the paradigm shift necessary for our evolution. Everything in our life is all about our mindset and can be applied to any experience and situation within our existence. Remember, you always have a choice, and many times that logical choice will be to change your perception. One of the most important mindset changes we can bring is that of self-perception.

This has to start with how we see ourselves, the projections made onto us as children, and continuing throughout our existence. Not many of us grow to be balanced adults and that is largely due to our experiences as children. We were shamed, made to feel guilt, perhaps made to feel small by others, and repeatedly made to feel unworthy and undeserving.

This is why we must go back to our childhood and heal our inner child so we can bring the changes to ourselves and evolve. Many of us struggle with our self-esteem and are unable to truly love ourselves. We will not be able to love someone else unconditionally if we don't have love for ourselves.

As we heal our childhood, we allow room to trust and believe in ourselves, and putting all this together, we can love ourselves. The inner healing we do will bring a change in perspective with the ability and capacity to know we are worthy and deserving of our own love, as well as from others.

Once we have determined a need for growth and evolution, the best place to start would be a new mindset with determination and dedication. If we truly desire to be good at anything, we must choose to go the extra step, or face mediocrity. That's not necessarily a bad thing—being average—but all it takes is one additional step to be extraordinary.

When we choose to be average, we have limited ourselves on many levels, creating blocks on our evolution. The stagnation we have created is also known as our comfort zone, and we find an inability to grow or evolve. Our need to be the person that we are authentically should be enough to feed our evolution, and perhaps settling for who we are would be enough for some. Remember, we are limitless BEings.

Choosing a new mindset takes some kind of plan and vision of a future that we can be successful within. This is perhaps born out of a need to know more, be more, out of want for more or better for ourselves. Regardless of what drives us, our desire for more facilitates a new mindset. This process is one of perpetual change and acceptance with a higher degree of determination.

What is involved with making a new mindset? How do we choose our new direction? What is the first step and how do we take it? All good questions to ask, and the answers lie within the spirit self, not the 3D self. Now that we have recognition of the need for a better version of ourself, our intention needs action.

Intention without action is just another meaningless word. Putting action to our intention brings direction and forward movement. This is much the same as the tradition of a New Year's resolution. We have the best intention with our statement, and often the follow-through is limited as we lose interest and desire to accomplish our task for various reasons—mainly a lack of motivation and self-discipline.

This shows us the need for determination and dedication. Most resolutions are short lived, as are the reasons for a new mindset. Only you can better yourself and only you limit yourself. Sure, there will always be circumstances that are limiting, but there are always ways to work around them if we choose. Remember, we always have choice.

So, how do we work around circumstance? We have incredibly creative spirit guides who will show us those ways if we choose to listen and allow them to fulfill their purpose. This is where trust and belief in ourselves comes into play. Our intuition is our guides speaking to us, and we truly need to trust what we feel and hear from them, and not ignore them.

I know I spent many years ignoring the inner dialogue of my guides and made it extremely hard for them to succeed in their efforts. Sometimes it takes a traumatic event to shake us out of this pattern and to have understanding of their importance on our Awakening Journey. Mine came through awareness of self-sabotaging patterns before I was able to learn my lessons.

Implementing a new mindset takes courage and strength, and I admire those who choose this life-altering decision. I know the difficulty in bringing the necessary changes, but I also understand the need to bring those changes with allowance. Once again, we're back to desire and need for a better life. It's truly one of the best gifts we can give ourselves.

Now that we have made up our mind that change is necessary, we go within and find the courage and strength by allowing trust for the self. This is a huge change in pattern and belief for many of us, as the childhood projections created blocks in our natural ability to trust and believe in ourselves. This dynamic of trust and belief will become the very foundation upon which our Awakening Journey is built.

There can be no evolution without them, and therefore no forward movement. Find reasons to bring them to the forefront instead of reasons for self-doubt. Look for ways to overcome the self-doubt we're so good at and become good at self-respect and love instead. Don't give yourself less than what you deserve.

Knowing we are indeed worthy and deserving of trusting and believing in ourselves is a major pattern and belief paradigm. Many of us have believed for the majority of our lives we are not worthy or deserving of better, and have settled for much less than is our birthright.

This is one of the first mindsets we should consider as we step into a better version of ourselves, and truly, one of the most profound changes we can bring to our lives. We deserve our own love and respect—an obvious birthright given to us by the Divine—as well as to trust and believe in ourselves.

Happiness is a choice we make daily and also a birthright, to feel good about ourselves instead of the constant self-doubt that has been projected onto us since early childhood. Personally, I got tired of not liking myself or being able to love myself, and that was what facilitated my need for a better version of myself.

Back in the 1980s there was a movement referred to as the "New Age Movement" which brought a strong foundation for what became "spirituality." I read about 10 pages of a book and saw a very basic and simple outline for what has become the "Age of Awakening." One thing I took from that time was something that has stuck with me all these years.

That one simple thought was that we reinvent ourselves every day. This means that every day we do something, take one step to becoming the person we know ourselves to be, allowing ourselves to bring a necessary change toward our evolution as a conscious decision. This is a conscious effort we need to make every day of our lives.

Once we have chosen to believe we have completed any effort, we stop evolving. That process will follow us through every future life because we have chosen to end the patterns of sabotaging our journey, allowing growth that is never-ending. Any time we believe we are finished with a task we immediately end the process of evolution.

Choosing to allow a fresh mindset opens many doors of opportunity for learning, growing, and healing. It brings more new ideas and an openness to the changes necessary to our Awakening Journey and to becoming our authentic self. Openness to change can and will have major impacts on our spiritual and personal lives.

Can you honestly give yourself a logical and acceptable reason not to be a better person? It's the gift that keeps on giving!!! I'm not talking about materialistic goods, as those exist outside the realm of spirituality and are strictly a 3D concept. I'm talking about allowing yourself the opportunity to evolve spiritually and personally to a higher standard of BEing.

It's the difference between choosing to step into another dimension or remain within a stagnant existence. Many teachers of spirituality often mention "an attitude of gratitude" as a way of life. This means the more gratitude we give, the more we will have to give gratitude for. Again, this is not materialistic. There are more ways to be rich outside of money and possessions.

Indeed, we all desire a life of comfort and abundance, but on our Awakening Journey, the abundance comes in more personal ways. A few would be: An abundance of love (whether giving or receiving), like-minded BEings we share our journey with, a life fulfilled with beauty and light, and a clear conscience. Most of us enjoy knowing our hard work and efforts have paid us handsomely with such things as I have mentioned.

It comes down to what is truly important to us on our spiritual, or Awakening, and healing journeys. Personally, I find my gratification in knowing that I have worked hard to achieve this Higher Dimensional existence. Anyone who has excelled in their field has earned their station and taken their rightful place of distinction. Their determination and dedication of pursuit has brought them to a place deserving of their efforts.

You make the choice, you make the effort, therefore, you reap the rewards, so to speak. We will only get out of life what we put into our efforts. If you are willing to take that extra step every day, you will see your efforts have taken you beyond possibility. If we derive satisfaction simply doing enough to get by on, then this is how our life will be.

To reach our untapped potential and take ourselves beyond our imagination, we need to choose maximum effort. This is how we become our authentic self, and this is how we realize all the dreams we ever had, through determination and dedication. So, what is your choice? This is what your life will become. Choose well.

Chapter 5

Self-Mastery

On our Awakening Journey there is much talk about self-mastery. This is such an important necessity, but what is it and what does it mean? Self-mastery is a multi-layered process of going within the self and knowing you through a deep, intense journey of discovery, tearing back layers of personal untapped potential, and healing the darkest recesses of the self. The journey inward will be difficult, sometimes scary, and a beautiful means of expression of the innermost BEing. It won't be easy, but nothing worthy of success ever is.

I truly believe everything we will ever need is already within us, and a common purpose that of those on an Awakening Journey share. It can be a beautiful adventure filled with mystery and intrigue, or it can become your worst nightmare, depending on how you perceive it. You will navigate your deepest, darkest fears and wonder at the joy of discovering your own beauty that was previously not noticed and acknowledged. You are indeed a limitless BEing capable of so much more than you could ever believe.

Sadly, we have never been taught how to approach the many processes within our Awakening, which makes navigating our journey difficult at best. This book is written from an Awakening perspective and is meant to be a guide to learning how to thrive in every aspect of your life as you are guided by your spirit self. The journey within is not dependent on the outside world, rather trusting and believing in the self with love, grace, mercy, and acceptance.

The journey to Awakening is not a new concept, nor recently discovered within modern spirituality. The Egyptians, Chinese, Native indigenous tribes, and certainly the Essenes spoke of the Awakening Journey thousands of years ago. They had a deep understanding of the metaphysical world we are just now rediscovering and knew the value of the relationship with the self, the Earth, and the Universe. They knew how to manipulate energy, heal the body, and could harness environmental elements.

They understood how to use gems, crystals, and precious metals for their innate properties of healing. Other such noted groups and individuals who used their knowledge also include Shamans, Druids, witches, alchemists, and Holy men of all beliefs and cultures. One thing they all had in common was an openness to accept their own inner Divinity and acceptance of being an unlimited entity.

We are rediscovering so much of what ancient cultures and civilizations practiced in their everyday life. Mathematics, philosophy, science, physics, just to name a few concepts we use today, were born out of those past civilizations. They understood astrology and astronomy, charted stellar movements, predicted eclipses, and the many ways we are affected by the moon and Sun. They planted and harvested by the moon and kept track of seasons and the passing of time by the rising and falling of the moon.

So, why are so many just now hearing about the ancient ways? I say, because many of us have come here at this time to bring back the ways of the old, bringing change to an out-of-control civilization, reliant on force through the means of fear and control. We are here at this time to usher in the Divine Feminine Energy and bringing the necessary change out of a patriarchal society, and into balance.

And this has exactly what to do with self-mastery and the Awakening Journey? Everything. There is so much more to human BEings than what we believe. Historically, mankind has been suppressed by leaders controlling the masses, making sure we are kept ignorant of the meaning of freedom. The time is right, with modern technology to spread corrective measures, ensuring our very evolution out of the darkness, brought by thousands of years of control.

We all volunteered to come here at this time to bring back the ancient ways, ending the enslavement of humanity to the needs of the few. We are bound by Universal Laws first observed by Hermes Trismegistus and abide by the laws of modern man. Many of the principles we live by came from early civilizations such as the Greeks and Romans, laying the foundations of our societies.

What does this have to do with us? A shared and common purpose is to bring awareness of these past cultures back to mainstream thought, breaking down the walls and barriers built by world leaders to keep us in a state of fear. Mankind is easier to control when they live in fear of retribution by controlling factions. Living outside of their projected fears is just one area we will learn to incorporate on our journey of Awakening. We are meant to trust and believe in ourselves and that has been buried in past cultures and civilizations.

Why is it necessary for us to practice self-mastery? Simply because we are much more than we believe. We all have within us much untapped potential that goes beyond accepted societal and personal beliefs. We are truly limitless BEings when we are aligned with The Divine, living a heart-centered existence. I have often stated in this book my beliefs of limitlessness and will bring understanding on how to become closer to the authentic self, the Spirit. We can all adapt from each other's knowledge and wisdom, learning how to incorporate beyond concepts, making them reality.

I will say often that everything begins with awareness and recognition, being the basis of knowledge. Wisdom is nothing more than knowing how to use our knowledge for our benefit.

Many of us will find intrigue with "new methods" and have every intention of bettering ourselves, but without action, intention is just another word.

We must take an active measure with our intentions for them to come to their fruition, with a proposed and desired outcome. We can read all the books, watch all the videos, and have understanding of the concepts, but until we put them to use, they will still be a concept. Action will take it from being a concept to a useful part of our lives. Again, awareness is the beginning of this process and that awareness is always of the self first.

Self-mastery is knowing the whys and hows that make up our personality and BEing. Why did I react or respond as I did? Why was I triggered? What was the trigger? As we journey inward, we will find all the answers we search for. Always remember, we already possess all we need. Books and the experiences of others can bring reference points, but we are looking for our own truth, not someone else's.

Your truth lies within you, not them, and the only way to know your truth is to go within and find it. It is the process of discovering all that you have locked away in order to live. Our birthright is bliss and it is more of a goal than a state of being. We will find many struggles as we journey inward and the concept of constant bliss unfortunately brings a denial of what we don't want to face about ourselves.

Our journey will be filled with highs and lows that we need to learn to navigate in an attempt to balance and juggle all aspects of the self. Some are good, some bad, some delightful, some downright scary. It is only through acceptance that we can see truth outside of our perception. There will always be a better way, but it may be the hardest way and we need to accept the good with the bad. We simply cannot deny what we don't like about ourselves and our lives, only wanting to see what pleases us and brings us comfort.

It is acceptance of the self as we are that will allow us to proceed on our inward journey. We are a constant work in progress as we are constantly changing, transcending our every yesterday. Adapting to those changes is key, and that allowance of change within our mindset will bring us beyond what we believe we know and have accepted as comfortable and normal.

Self-mastery is allowing yourself to change projected patterns and beliefs, undoing years of control by others, making sure we conform to their ideals, beliefs, and being told who to be. As I have stated often, we must undo all that has been done to us, as we journey toward our authentic self. The belief of who we are is not who we truly are. It has all been projected onto us from birth.

As we evolve on our Awakening Journey, we must make the necessary changes. Getting to know yourself as you are, not who you've been forced to be, is truly a wonderful adventure of self-discovery, and although it is not easy, it doesn't have to be hard. Accept that there must be change. Take a step, any step, to begin. If we don't make that first move, there will be no evolution.

Within you is the strength, courage, and wisdom to move forward, so let's go find it! Trust and belief in yourself are crucial, so change your mindset and start trusting and believing in you again. Look into yourself and find the areas you believe should be processed first, taking careful stock of what you like and dislike about yourself. That is a wonderful first step in this process. Take a real hard look at you and prioritize your findings.

Make a hard copy if you need to, as it will bring a reference point for the remainder of the process, but don't stick to what you feel as absolute truth. Remain open and willing to change your priorities, because you'll definitely change your mind the more you get to know you. What you believed were your strengths could easily be your weaknesses, and vice versa.

Now that you have begun to take a peek within, don't allow yourself to talk down to you. That serves as self-sabotage and will only impede your efforts as it is counterproductive. Simply make notes, whether mental or on paper, and know those will always change with discovery. This next statement is highly important to your efforts of self-mastery.

GIVE YOURSELF PERMISSION TO LET GO OF ALL ATTACHMENTS AND EXPECTATIONS IN HOW YOU PERCEIVE YOURSELF AND YOUR LIFE. You have allowed yourself to be defined by the projections of others, regardless of how much you like yourself or not, and have attachment to those definitions. You have been given expectations by others to set your own standard of who you are. It's time to be you, and you must be willing to let all that go in order to be authentic.

How do you define yourself? By what standards are you living your life? Are they your standards or those of others? To begin with, stop seeing yourself in the 3D and accept your inner Divinity and that you are a spirit in a body, not a body with a spirit. I know how difficult it can be to change that particular mindset because it goes against everything we have been taught.

If you feel as if this is a mind-blowing concept, then take time to allow it to sink in. Absorb it and embrace it. This step is one we cannot omit from the process, as it begins the change in mindset you need. Your freedom lies in the balance, so embrace this new pattern and belief. Once you have fully accepted this paradigm, you will begin to see from a new perspective.

Remember that I said to not allow yourself to be attached to how you see yourself. This acceptance should open you to so many new and wonderful processes, and it also helps you align with the spirit self. The 3D self, at this point, should no longer be allowed to be in charge of any process. This is taking your wounded ego out of the lead and allowing the heart to take over, as it is meant to be.

This first part of the process may take time to believe and implement.

There is no time limit on self-mastery as we are always a work in progress, so know it is not an event and nothing will happen with the snap of fingers. Now we must incorporate patience into our new mindset. Patience has been one of the hardest lessons for me to learn because it entails letting go of the illusion that you control your life. Sorry, sunshine, you have already contracted for all of your experiences and what life brings.

Changing our perception of ourselves is a turn toward changing how we believe we need to be, not as we are. Say, for instance, do you see yourself as unattractive, perhaps you say you're stupid, perhaps you believe yourself to be so weak that there can never be any change for the better. The cellular self takes your every thought and word as gospel truth, so we must change how we speak to ourselves. At this time on our journey—more than any other time—we have to learn how to be self-loving and respectful.

We can no longer talk down to the self for any reason, not even jokingly. If you don't give yourself the opportunity to overcome these projected patterns and beliefs, you will maintain that status quo and there will be no forward movement. We have to learn that all the negative things others have projected onto us, especially through words and actions, are not ours and never were.

We can no longer allow others to keep putting us down, making us feel small and unworthy, treating us with disrespect. It all starts with the love and respect you deserve, coming from you. If you don't allow yourself to treat you as such, it will follow that you won't allow others to either. All of these healthy boundaries necessary for you must begin with you. We must, at this point, be the parents to ourselves that we needed as children.

The wounded ego is, in fact, the wounded inner child. They both stopped developing at a certain age for most of us, as the inner child was pushed away and made to feel unwanted. The inner child was denied the nurturing it believed it needed, and as it tried to express itself, was unfortunately pretty well shut down before the age of six.

The wounded ego will always exist in the belief of lack. It will always tell you that life is about you, you're not receiving enough, and will undoubtedly react with anger if allowed to roam free and be in charge. That is the exact response of a child, because they don't normally have the ability to see beyond their own needs. So many adults are still in this same mindset and will never develop beyond this stage.

Many mindsets and realizations are going to be made within the first few months of your journey of Awakening. Allow yourself time to let these discoveries sink in and don't allow yourself to become overwhelmed by these newfound ways. There will always be some amount of inner conflict, but it doesn't have to be tumultuous.

As I stated earlier, we must allow ourselves to be open to change, and open to the allowance to change. It is one of the only constants on your journey and to deny yourself change could be damning to your journey. Most of us are incredibly set in our ways and closed off to anything new that may take us out of our comfort zone and into a state of vulnerability. Your comfort zone is why you're stuck and unable to move forward, and the state of vulnerability is the only state in which we can grow.

Your comfort zone contains every attachment and expectation you have allowed yourself to be defined within and by. The key here is to take that first step we talked about earlier, stepping outside the box you have made for yourself or allowed someone else to put you within. Once we step outside of that box and our comfort zone, we see that we are in fact limitless BEings and undefinable by any 3D construct or limitation.

That first step you just took may appear to be tiny, but is the biggest and most important step toward your authentic self. Do you feel anxiety and fear as you walk away from your own limitations? That feeling of vulnerability is freedom and not what we need to fear. We need to fear being locked within a box with no chance of forward movement and evolution.

We are not afraid to fail, as most of us have learned to be comfortable with failure and have become quite good at it. We are more afraid of success because many of us are unsure of how it feels to not be in a state of lack. I have always said about myself, "I've never had money and really wouldn't know how to act if I did." It's really not important to me as I live comfortably within my means.

So, how do we transcend the feeling of lack? We allow ourselves to stop surviving and being a victim to want and need, and change our perspective to see that what we want and need, for the most part, are material goods meant to bring us comfort. Our lives before this discovery of forward progress have been built around having objects and belongings that are designed to bring us comfort, including some of the people in our lives.

In reality, all we are doing is reassessing our lives and changing our priorities of desires projected onto us, with the illusion that the one who dies with the most toys wins. The spiritual and Awakening Journeys are of the spirit, not the material. Sure, we all have some attachments to objects, but when you have taken your last breath of this incarnation, does it truly have meaning? Furthermore, can you take those objects with you into the next life? I have never seen someone who has transitioned actually take an object with them. It'll be there long after they expire.

All of the mindset changes we need to make are really quite simple. It's allowing yourself to make these mindset changes that is the difficult part. I found many years ago, the only way to bring change is to allow it, and that is one of the most important changes we can make for ourselves. I truly believe the openness to change can and will bring change. It also takes determination and dedication to be successful in any endeavor we undertake.

Now, I feel a need to ask you, the reader, this one question: Are you open to allowing change within your life and your personal world? If your answer is no, then you may want to check your priorities and see if you truly want to go further in your life, or if you're happy where you are with no desire for forward movement. If your current status is good enough for you, then that is where you will remain.

If you can honestly say without a shadow of doubt that you are willing to embrace change, then I urge you to continue reading, even if you need to put down this book in order to process and assimilate what you are remembering. I'm not telling you anything you don't know. I'm simply helping you remember. If you are not willing to change, then please at least allow the seeds planted within you to grow.

When we feel we can't, then we won't, and if we know we can, then we will—at least to some degree. Either way we are right and that pretty much defines us where we are right here, right now.

This is also a necessary mindset we all need to make within. With the attitude of "I can't" we have just limited ourselves and stopped trusting and believing in ourselves. I will say though, "I can't" is the biggest block we can face and it will always stop us dead in our tracks.

Now the pertinent question is," Why do I believe I can't?" We will need to look really close at ourselves and understand why we have this belief. What series of events took place that allowed this fear-based thought process to dominate us? When did I stop trusting and believing in myself? The journey now begins with a need to answer these questions and we take another step toward our authentic self. Perhaps this is a result of years of projections of others, usually beginning with the immediate family.

How often have been you told you "can't", stopping you from even trying? When we are told we "Can't" is it because it is illegal, not possible, or a projection of someone else's limitations? If we never ask, or never try, then the answer will always be no, and we'll never know if we could. Having the understanding of why we believe something, has the ability to allow us to change that particular mindset, pattern, and belief.

When we question everything, we have the ability to see it as the observer, allowing us to bypass the wounded ego and see beyond our perception. As the observer, we detach emotionally and have the ability to see truth instead of perception. I use this process often, especially at the end of my day as I look back to see where I could have improved my responses and reactions.

As the observer, we have no personal attachment, and we have the ability to step outside our ego. Remember, the wounded ego is the wounded inner child. We should not ignore it, but neither can we allow it to be in charge. The balanced and healed ego is indeed one of the best allies we have on our Awakening Journey, allowing us to access the heart brain, living in alignment with our spirit and inner Divinity.

How does any of this help me go within? It helps because it is a new awareness of the self. The process of self-awareness will last lifetimes once begun and carried out with determination and dedication. How well do you really know yourself? Why do you like your favorite color? Why don't you like that particular song? Why does that person bring out the best or worst in you?

We can't honestly answer any of these questions without much self-reflection. Self-mastery is intensely studying our own personal nuances, all of our quirks and quims, while discovering why we've become who we are. Do you honestly remember why you're afraid of dogs, or why you have any fear you have? The only way to know is through the process of self-mastery.

How far within you go is your free will, as is how much you dedicate to your journey. But ask yourself these questions: Am I honestly happy with the person that I AM? Can I be even happier being a more complete version of myself? Am I truly happy with who I AM, or do I fear knowing myself and my darkness? You're the only one who can answer these, and you're the only one who can make yourself a better version.

Always remember it's your life, your journey. Please also remember you came here for reasons possibly unknown to you at this time. Those purposes will come to you as you need to know them, when you are ready to fulfill one and begin another. You raised your hand when the Universe asked for volunteers and you chose this incarnation for reasons beyond your knowing at this time.

I will say this, though: You owe it to yourself to be the best version of you possible, not settling for anything less than what you deserve worthy of. You have nothing to lose and everything to gain by allowing your journey to be what it's meant to be, achieving many untapped potentials within you.

All you have to do is trust and believe in yourself, with a desire to be more than what you know. Connecting to your inner Divinity, your spirit self, is a key step to endless possibilities. Allowing yourself to be guided by your spirit self and living a heart-based existence are a strong foundation toward spiritual and personal growth. Openness to change can and will bring change itself.

For those of you who feel a need to change the world, you are quite capable and have within you all the resources you need. How do you change the world? You do it by bringing change to yourself. If enough of us better ourselves, there will eventually be an Event Horizon and the world will have no choice but to follow us.

It is contagious to others when they see how we have changed ourselves for the better. They do have recognition and their natural curiosity will enable them to want to do whatever it is you're doing, at least begin to question themselves. Perhaps you've sparked a fire under someone who is stuck in a place, not knowing how to get over their stagnation.

You've just facilitated change within that other person who noticed you've changed, and they will do the same for someone else. It becomes a snowball effect and you've just helped others to be a better version of themselves. We never truly know how we affect the lives of others. Shine your loving light bright and proud and dare to be a trendsetter.

They will see how happy you are and want a huge helping of whatever you're doing. Without pushing your personal agenda, plant all the seeds you can, just by your example. You don't have to say anything to anyone, and in fact, we shouldn't, unless asked. Simply lead by example and those meant to follow will.

Your personal journey within will be noticed by others, and it's not necessary to tell others your business unless they want to know. Our Awakening Journey is quite private, but the need to talk with other like-minded BEings will always exist. Put your wish out to the Universe and quietly wait for them to come to you as it's meant to be.

TRUST. As we evolve, others who match our vibration will be brought to us, and before you know it, you'll have a spiritual family. You'll help each other evolve and others will see your evolution and sense your new frequencies. TRUST. They will come when you are ready. Change will come when you are ready. Just allow it to happen organically, but do your part.

…Always and in all ways

Trust and believe

In yourself…

Chapter 6

Perception

The dictionary defines perception as "a judgement resulting from awareness or understanding." Our Awakening Journey finds us expanding this to a much deeper and meaningful definition, as it goes beyond the normal accepted idea. Our perception, in fact, is based upon our personal experiences and beliefs, and unfortunately for most of us, it is predicated to the wounded ego point of view and often skewed.

I truly believe our perception has the ability to change our personal and spiritual self drastically for our highest good. I have changed my life entirely just by changing how I see life and what it brings me. Just like many of you reading this, I was used to how I was told life should be, who I was told to be, and even what I was told I should believe.

It wasn't until I accepted myself and my Awakening Journey that I could see I had to walk away from all of that. I realized, I was not any of what was projected onto me, and it was up to me and me alone to make the changes within myself and become authentic. I had to not only change my mindset, but my perception and way of thinking to become the real me, not an avatar of what others expected me to be.

I had to go within my own darkness, find my courage, strength, and will, and with dedication, do what I had to do: Walk away from all that I was and all I thought I knew. I discovered, by allowing myself to buy into the societal need of controlling me to fit into the little box of confinement given to me at birth, I had become nothing more than an automaton of regulated beliefs.

That was hard to accept at first, but I soon caved into my spirit need of non-conformity toward authenticity, and when I found allowance, I knew there would be no turning back. The only path for me was forward and upward, as my journey of discovery demanded that I turn my focus inward, and allow my spirit self to guide me, as I navigated this destructive and necessary phase of my journey.

Having awareness brings recognition, and armed with intention, I took the first step toward my evolution of authenticity. I accepted the fact that I was not me, which brought one of the most important questions I could ask myself: *Who am I?* Having decided the best answer to that question being, *certainly not who I currently am*, I then found myself asking this: *Am I who I want to be or truly am?* The only answer I could logically find was a resounding *hell no.*.

So, how was I to become my authentic self? Quite simply, my answer was, by unbecoming their version of me. This is a huge undertaking—this unbecoming—because it meant I had to use my perception in deciding to become either who I wanted to be, or who I was meant to be. I was still, at this point, being led by my wounded ego who demanded I be who I wanted to be. We, my ego and spirit self, fought many internal battles from that day forward, and it was on.

Armed with my newfound courage and strength, I took the challenge. I set out to discover who I was meant to be. I began to separate myself consciously from their "projected me" self, learning to change projected patterns and beliefs. I had to allow the storm within to rage, regardless of how intense it would become. I had been through a lot to this point and could never imagine what was to come.

I chose to see this challenge as an inward adventure instead of an arduous task, changing my perspective. I allowed myself to see this as opportunity to learn, heal, and grow rather than being a victim, living in survival mode due to their efforts of control. *But how could I possibly find the good within this?* I chose to ask myself instead, *how could I not?*

There will always be a silver lining to every cloud if we simply choose to see it, rather than just the cloud. The ability to see the bigger picture will bring us out of that very survival need and secure us in a place to be successful. That perspective also enables us to bring a different mindset, allowing ourselves to rise above and beyond victim mentality.

Now, I was truly ready to move forward in allowing myself to become authentic and the mindset had been made. I was more determined than ever, and the spirit self did step up and guide me to a new sense of awareness of not only life, but the scope of my Awakening Journey. There was absolutely no one and no thing going to stand in my way.

I began to view much of what I believed I thought I knew as extra baggage and soon the weight of toxic beliefs and patterns began falling away. I had to start seeing myself in a new way of love and compassion in order to begin loving, trusting, and believing in myself. The memories of so many hateful and hurtful words came at me in torrents. I gave them forgiveness and love, allowing them to exist one more time, as I sat within the pain and trauma of each one, allowing them to be healed.

A continuous flow ensued, as I allowed movement from deep within where I had pushed them all down, until there was nowhere left for me. My all-consuming self-hatred had to somehow be converted to self-love and respect and I knew the only way for this to happen was to dig deep, finding the roots and where it began in the early stages of my childhood development. I had to face all those years of projections and programming and unbecome all I had become.

The fire within had become an all-out war with my spirit and the shattered bubble of my wounded ego, with the realization that I no longer had to give my energy to the past. I couldn't allow myself to believe their truths any longer. My mission became the search for my truth, building my legacy, and finding my authentic self.

Every day brought more pain than the previous day but I encouraged myself to keep facing that pain. I knew the only way out was into the recesses of the darkness I feared the most, right on through to where I was the light. I didn't fully understand how I was to proceed, but I had to start somewhere and take some measure forward. I isolated myself from everyone and everything and began to feel empowered.

I knew I had to figure out the processes to allow the healing to begin. I did have understanding that I would have to offer myself the unconditional love I deserved with the utmost self-respect. I couldn't even look into a mirror at this point in my life because I hated that person looking back at me. So, I lifted my eyes and looked deep within my very core and uttered a meek "I love you." *There, I said it.*

I spent many hours crying, purging, and releasing any pain I could bring forth, only to feel lost within my darkness, but I never caved into my ego which screamed for me to stop. I was now at a point of no return and allowed it to flow at will. I surrendered my need for control and asked The Divine to please take what I could no longer endure. Suddenly, I felt it all leave and a stillness overcame me, a peace within I had never felt before.

I had just hit upon the very salvation I sought... surrender. I had one of the biggest "ah-ha" moments of my life with this change in my perception. All I really needed to do from the onset was to change my mindset and allow myself to surrender. This new belief would end up shattering the old useless pattern of believing the illusion that I was in control. Wow... mind blown... I'm not in control.

We all have been taught from an early age that we have to be in control of our lives in every aspect. I know many of you, as well as myself, found it hard to believe someone or something was in control of my life. Indeed!!! Did this revelation mean that I was simply a pawn in a game, meant to just take what life brought? Absolutely not.

I believe we have free will, which is something many do not believe in. So, then does this mean we are all predestined, as in fate? Indeed, we all signed a soul-contract that would define each experience we would see, but we are never powerless as fate would imply. We are in charge of our responses, reactions, emotions, thoughts, words, and actions, with an innate ability to change our life.

We have the ability, through choice, to change our lives by what comes from us. How we respond and react to any given situation or experience will set in motion what comes next, and that is our ability to bring change. We choose to either allow ourselves to be a victim, or we choose to see an opportunity to better ourselves.

That is free will. We always have a choice, even in the most extreme situation.

I had learned how to break free from projected beliefs and patterns. It is through awareness of these old patterns and beliefs that I now had recognition to stop my current thought process and implement the new. This is a major step on our journey toward our authentic self and how we unbecome who and what we were. Sounds simple enough.

Now, when I recognize the old, I replace it with the new. I found amazing liberation with the realization that I no longer had to be a slave to the confinement of a projected existence. I was ecstatic within my newfound paradigm shift, and I would utilize this process, and my freedom was now within reach. I could see light where I had seen nothing but darkness, and that light was me.

I slowly began to focus my awareness to bring every change I could within. Finally, I started to see life differently and with a new understanding. All I had to do was allow myself to see a different perspective, and a new way would present itself to me. If I had only known this before, when I believed I had to suffer needlessly. Pain is inevitable, but suffering is an option and a choice.

Our suffering comes from not being able to accept what is, because we are locked into the same old mindset that brought us to where we are. Knowing I had choice made all the difference in my world, and I would now choose to respond and not react. Not an easy mindset to change, but definitely manageable and doable.

I had begun to see the choices I had everywhere I looked and suddenly it became almost like a very fun game where I could always win. Yeah, I still made bad decisions, but now I wasn't locked into my decisions, and I could change course midstream and make necessary corrections. I learned just because I made a decision, it didn't have to be etched in stone.

I would learn to forgive myself for not knowing better, and I learned what self-love and respect was, and learned how to give that to myself and receive it as well. We must allow ourselves to receive as well as give, because they are a continuation of each other, with the same measure of grace and acceptance.

I have used this principle of perspective through my journey and have found many ways to change my life for the better. I vowed to always try and see the big picture instead of my narrow-minded vision. Do I always succeed? Absolutely not. I have learned to allow myself to make mistakes and not try to be perfect.

I have learned that just because I see things a certain way, doesn't mean that my perception is right in truth. I see now that I have to look at every situation from as many different angles as I can, and allow the understanding that my truth is not absolute, nor will it ever be. There is always a higher truth to be found, but I will always stand in my truth until a higher one is presented, and I am always open to that higher truth.

I have learned to know the difference in a response or reaction from my ego, and work daily toward healing and balancing the wounded ego. I allow myself to be a "work in progress" and know that I must trust the process every step of the way. This has done well to teach me patience, for I must allow the process to be what it is meant to be, not my expectations.

All of this has taught me how to trust and believe in myself and how to love me unconditionally. I will always work tirelessly to be my authentic self, unbecoming all that I am not. I have learned to allow life to happen and come to me as it is meant, not how I want it to be. Now, I have found a peace within that I never would have, had I not stumbled upon the word "surrender".

I have learned through this that the only way I can better myself is to become the change I need, and I am the only one who can. I am becoming my authentic and limitless self and know this is a journey and not an event, and I embrace any opportunity to be me... unconditional love.

Our perceptions, as I stated before, normally come from a wounded ego or an inner child needing to be heard. They both basically stopped developing during early childhood development, when we became someone other than our authentic self through projections from the outer world, which took us away from our inner self and our Divinity.

We didn't know any better as children, wanting to trust and be accepted by everyone and everything. Our mental development was in a very young stage, and we simply didn't have the knowledge we have now, so trust was really all we had. Ideally, we need to bring much forgiveness for our former self for many things, with unconditional love.

This is how we begin to heal the inner child, also very necessary on our healing journey. Knowing the difference between egoic and spirit perception means we must know ourselves on a deep level. This is, in part, self-mastery, and is indeed part of our Awakening Journey. Learning discernment will assist us on so many levels as we evolve.

We have three inner dialogues: The ego, the inner child, and the Divine self. Knowing which voice is in our ear is imperative, as two mock the one we need to listen to. The ego doesn't like change, the inner child wants to play and be heard, and the Divine voice needs us to evolve. It's not hard to know your own energy, but necessary to discern which voice is speaking.

There are many processes happening simultaneously through the process of self-mastery as well as the Awakening Process, mostly on a subconscious level, bringing us to where we need to be. The 3D doesn't have to know everything happening in our lives, and sometimes, we're better off accepting this. The 3D perception has a habit of bringing drama and trauma in its efforts to control.

We need to listen to the Divine self—with absolute trust in this voice—for guidance concerning our lives outside of the mundane everyday experiences. Choosing to allow the self to be guided by the Divine, rather than the ego, will save us much unnecessary drama and suffering.

This new mindset we are creating is choosing for our perceptions to come from the Divine self, or spirit self. This shift is a process of constant change with allowance for what is meant to be, away from what we want it to be. This stepping away from the 3D thought process brings us to our authentic self and state of BEing. This is the heart-centered self, bringing a new awareness and perspective to every aspect of our life.

Since the spirit-self brings us what is meant for our highest good, we should indeed allow it to lead us on our journey. We need to trust the knowing it brings and allow our perception to come from that higher place. The ego would rather we stay within the comfort zone it has created for us, not allowing us to evolve or become the authentic self.

There are many other ways we change our perspective, just through a deeper awareness. Many led by the ego believe everything is about themselves and make it about themselves, unable to see beyond the narrow scope of the wounded ego. They have been stuck there, and for many, have been for several lifetimes.

Learning to step outside of the self takes patience and time, but we will be richly rewarded once we know how. We become the observer, looking from a different angle, better able to see truth as it exists, not as we believe we see it. Allowing the spirit to guide us is achieved by listening to our Divine voice within.

Unfortunately for many of us, our perception is skewed and determined by the ego. Do we have all the facts before us? Was there an intention we weren't aware of? What exactly was meant when it was said? Did I miss something important when I blinked or momentarily looked away when distracted? The ability to answer any or all of these questions can and will change our perception to fit truth as it occurred.

We all use voice inflections differently, and many times, how we hear their inflections is not how we use them. This may cause our ego to react in an adverse manner, creating an issue that doesn't exist. The same goes with our tone of voice. Someone may be speaking purely out of passion that we perceive as anger. Our perception doesn't always match their intention.

This is how arguments and disagreements happen and they are often avoidable when we step outside of our perception by understanding the intended presentation of the statement. I know first-hand my passion has been mistaken for anger and am guilty of mistaking their intention. I've learned to ask if I'm not sure, avoiding an unnecessary issue.

Simply ask if they are angry. We can't know if we don't ask. You could be saving your marriage, a friendship, your job, and possibly a life. Just because we have a perception doesn't mean it is truth in reality. Are you beginning to see why we need to step outside of our own perception? We can use this in any aspect of our lives, making a much better existence for ourselves.

I remember going to church when I was younger and everyone would talk about the sermon for days. I found it quite interesting when hearing others say what they heard, and it being different than what others heard. Our perceptions are always based upon our experiences and how we experienced them.

As I listened to the others speak, I realized we all came away with a different perception, even though we heard the same exact words. It was almost as if the pastor had given 75 different sermons at the same time. *Doesn't that mean that either I'm wrong, or they're wrong?* Not at all. No one was wrong. We all had a different experience from the same event.

We all walked away with a different perception because we all needed to hear what was important to us. The pastor may have used a different word to describe something than we would have. That different word brought an altogether different meaning to someone else. A different perception.

Unfortunately for many, they will feel a need to defend their perception to any degree, believing their perception to be absolute truth. Knowing that truth is not absolute in any aspect of life allows our truth to evolve and our self along with it. The openness to accept this fact saves us much drama and needless suffering and simplifies our life. I have found that many arguments could have been avoided if we both had just listened to the other.

Learning to listen, to hear, and not respond is just good communication. We're all good at speaking, but listening is the most important act in conversation. What we heard and what was actually said oftentimes are completely different. Questioning ourselves is always a good thing, as long as self-doubt is not included.

If you aren't sure of what they said, their intention, or meaning, then ask. Save the argument, save the disagreement, and save the drama if there is any way possible. Learning to have the awareness that we all perceive differently brings us the opportunity to allow others to be who they are. We don't know how their experiences have shaped their lives or what those experiences were.

Armed with these new awarenesses of how perceptions differ, we can begin to understand how we all are unique. We can't believe ourselves to be right all the time and allow the ego to lead. We miss out on actual truth when we don't allow an opportunity to learn from others and their perspectives.

Unfortunately, a new mindset has emerged within society. Many now believe that if we are not agreeable to the perception of others, it's wrong. This has gone to an extreme, not allowing others to be who they are or to believe what they believe. There is a trend to bring violence, even murder, simply because we can't agree. This is incredibly evident within the political arena and becoming acceptable behavior.

One of our birthrights is to believe our truth without persecution from those who do not share that truth. We have a right to our beliefs and to live our lives as we see fit. No one has a right to push their personal agenda, trying to force others to their will. This is a sign of the times as the forces of darkness try to hold on to an outdated way of living.

Do not engage with those who will force their beliefs. Simply walk away and don't give them your energy. The useless arguments and possible ensuing violence can be avoided by not reacting or replying. If they still pursue, by all means contact the proper authorities. We can no longer enable those demanding others be merely a puppet to them. We have certain inalienable rights set forth by our government to ensure our pursuit of happiness. Don't allow someone to steal those God-given rights.

Chapter 7

How Do We Go Within?

One of the biggest obstacles on our Awakening Journey is allowing ourselves to unlearn what we have been taught our entire existence, learning what wasn't taught to us. No one ever taught us how to heal emotionally, how to connect with our self, our inner child, or that we even needed to heal emotionally. Evolution is an absolute part of our journey and we won't be able to evolve if we can't take care of what's truly important within us.

Our journey is all about self-mastery and that has to begin with self-awareness, getting to know who we are and what our truth is. The following chapter is a guideline to self-awareness, and although what works for some doesn't work for others, you can adjust this into a working model for yourself and begin or continue your journey inward.

Everything on our journey has to begin with conscious awareness. What is conscious awareness? It is the ability to feel and have perception of all things related to the self and our immediate surroundings. To be consciously aware means we are paying attention to and recognizing all that we can, with all of our senses.

Imagine a baby in the learning stages of life where everything is discovery and how they study what they have just experienced. They look in awe and amazement at us and all that is around them. They begin to have awareness of their perceived reality with wonder, and they begin their thought process, even if they don't have words to give definition.

The lack of words doesn't stop them from beginning to understand and question all they see. If you have never given thought to being in a state of conscious awareness, then there is no discovery. We know we have five senses, which we use to experience life, but there is so much more to us than just five senses.

We have to put all of it together and somehow make sense of it enough to understand it. This may be frustrating for some, because we can't understand except from our own experience, and if we have never had the experience, then we don't know how to respond or react. We have no reference point and no way of discerning truth in reality.

Many of us have been taught since childhood that we have to put others first and that all of our needs are secondary. Indeed, we must be aware of others around us and our effect on them through our actions, words, and even our presence. What we are not told is that we must put our inner needs first. What we are not told is that we are not responsible for what others do. So many of us ended up feeling as if someone else's reaction to what we did was our fault. We learned to feel guilt for something we didn't do.

We are not taught that we are all accountable for our own actions, reactions, thoughts, words, and emotions. With this understanding, we can rid ourselves of guilt and stop shaming ourselves. Perhaps what we said to someone "made them mad," or we "made them feel small," and we were taught that their emotional response was our fault.

The truth is, what we said triggered them and their reaction is an emotional response from within themselves. We touched something inside them that needs healed. So often their reaction will be anger and rage, and they will project this onto us, and blame us for what they feel. No. Absolutely not. Their reaction is not our responsibility.

We didn't make them feel that. We didn't hold a gun to their head and tell them they needed to feel that emotion. They are accountable for their own emotions. Maybe we could have said it a different way, with a different tone of voice, and that would indeed be on us, but still, they were the ones triggered, and we all must own our triggers.

When we take responsibility for our own actions, reactions, responses, thoughts, words, and emotions, we have accepted and made ourselves accountable, owning up to our part in any experience or situation. Often, another's perception of us is not what our intention was and their perception is in error.

Oftentimes we say or do something with a specific intention and their perception of what we said or did is in error and the blame game starts. They get mad at us, start accusing us, and the whole situation suddenly becomes something that was not intended. All they had to do was ask us what we meant, but because they were triggered, we ended up in an argument, things were said that can't be taken back, and we wound up with a mess that can't be fixed.

I've seen this scenario break relationships that were good, and I've seen this scenario break the spirit of others, myself included. They had a reaction, often to a trigger that caused the situation, and suddenly someone was on the defensive because they, or we, felt that their entire being was put into question.

Our integrity, honor, and many times our lineage is going to be attacked because one of us was triggered. This is a typical unhealed ego response. The unhealed ego will be the first to respond in anger and rage, feeling as if they have been told something is wrong with them, and perhaps insulted. So often this is not the case in truth.

So how do we not respond in anger and rage when we feel we have just been called out for something that was said or done? Quite simply by choosing not to respond, perhaps at all at first, and having the realization that our response is eminent. So, with that realization, we stop ourselves from blurting out with the immediate emotional response of anger or rage.

With that realization, we can change that course of the scenario, save our dignity, and understand that we are responding to a trigger within ourselves, taking accountability for our actions and our response. Now we need to ask what was meant, what their intention was, and can we talk instead of arguing. Now, we have ended the blame game, possibly saving a relationship and/or friendship because of a misunderstanding. It is always a good idea if we are not sure of another's intentions to question what was meant.

This is how the process of conscious awareness works. Many of us have never thought to look at every aspect of ourselves and never had the ability to understand the logistics and workings of our inner self. This is exactly how we get to know ourselves and how we learn to utilize the process of self-mastery.

As with just about anything else on our Awakening Journey, once we have awareness, we can implement a change in perspective. By stopping our own response of anger or rage, we have changed our perspective of not only our self, but the situation, scenario, or experience. We can adapt this to every aspect of ourselves and our lives, changing ourselves and our life in the process.

How many times in our lives have we been in a situation where someone else's decision has had an effect on us, especially in a negative fashion? How did we respond at first? What was our emotional state upon realizing the impact on our life? How is that decision going to change our life? *Why do I have to experience this? Why is this happening to me? This is totally unfair to me. Why are they doing this at all? I hate that person...*

This is all coming from a victim mentality, and again, responses from an unhealed ego. They are all good questions, and now that there is some recognition, we can begin the process of stepping into a better quality of being. This is a really good place to realize the need to heal and balance the wounded ego, as we now have a definitive statement from the wounded ego. This is when we replace old patterns with new ones.

So, how do we step out of a victim mentality? Conscious awareness is, once again, the beginning of our perception and a change we need to make within ourselves. To step out of the victim mentality, we need to change the perception from a negative thought process to a positive one. A victim will always ask, *why is this happening to me*, as well as all the above-mentioned questions, feeling as if they have no choice and are locked into the situation.

Change the question from *why is this happening to me* to *what can I learn from this so I can learn, grow, and heal from it.* Now we have turned this around and made it positive. We can do this in every aspect of our lives and in the process turn our lives around for the better. A victim mentality is always a block because we have put up a wall with no chance of forward movement.

We are unable to thoroughly see any way out of our own thought process, so we have nowhere to go, and that is the block. We have made ourselves believe that no good can possibly come from the situation and we accept defeat or failure. I do have understanding that there are times when we are a victim and there is no possible good to come from anything we have experienced.

I was robbed at gun point and allowed myself to be the victim for a period of time, so I changed my perception, relived the experience in slow motion, and scrutinized every move. I remembered not everything is about me. But I still couldn't understand why this happened and why I was a part of this experience.

As I studied that scenario and my emotions, and felt into the robber's emotions, all I felt was raw fear coming from both of us. I wasn't sure if he was going to end my life right there, or even why I was chosen. I changed my perception and realized I wasn't chosen by him, I just happened to be the next person they came across, so I was just in the wrong place at the wrong time.

So, why did I need to experience this? *Why was this necessary?* Oh... victim mentality questions. *What did I learn from this?* I learned that we must experience both good and bad in life in order to grow, heal, and learn. Experiences are neutral. Our perception gives it definition of good or bad. *But how could I possibly grow and heal from this?*

It brought back past memories from when I felt absolute terror as a child. It triggered something inside of me that I needed to heal. The memory was from a particular incident as a child that to this day I can still see, but it brought me the opportunity to heal that childhood trauma, to offer forgiveness, and to understand why that happened as a child. I had to go back to that time, see it happen all over again, and try and make sense of it.

As I looked back, I asked myself, *why did he do what he did to that extreme?* I remembered what he had said about his childhood and his life, how he was raised, and how he was treated. His childhood was violent because his father could only respond in anger and rage, so in his eyes it was what he knew, and it was right because he was taught to be that way.

He didn't have the ability to change that pattern in his life and could not allow himself to see beyond what he knew, so he repeated those patterns throughout his life until he was older, and all he could do was look back at his life and see regret, without the ability to show remorse.

With a change in perception, he could have changed that pattern and changed the lives of those around him as well. But the fact is, when we experience bad in our lives, our reaction or response is our responsibility and our part in any bad experience or situation. Indeed, even though the experience is unprovoked, we have a part to play in it through our response or reaction.

It is the human condition to have an adverse reaction to a bad experience and there is where we apply our conscious awareness. We put ourselves under a microscope and analyze our process of response or reaction. Why did I respond or react as I did? Where did I learn to respond or react in this manner and could I have changed it?

Again, we respond from the memory of a past experience with similar happenings—a reference point. Once we search within ourself, we will eventually find a trigger and find what needs to be healed, taking us out of victim mentality and turning it around to be a benefit. We have the ability to now heal, learn, and grow from even the darkest of pain and trauma we have experienced.

We have taken yet another step in learning self-mastery. We have also brought about a change in perception, and possibly, changed an old pattern or belief. No one ever taught us to properly think things through, and so often we do not go deep enough, and are unable to see what we need to see in order to bring change.

We fall short of untapped potential and we are unable to be all we truly can be. With self-awareness there will always be recognition and there will always be a chance to grow, heal, and learn, allowing us to evolve and become our authentic limitless self. Discovering our truth within of who we are will change as we evolve, and we need to be vigilant of those changes.

The process of going within is acceptance of who we are, without judgment, coming from a place of unconditional love. We will see a bigger picture that needs focus on the minute aspects of the self. We need to examine all of our subtle nuances and understand the whys and hows of our existence.

When we begin to go within, we may see parts of ourselves in absolute horror, or a deep fondness through vivid memories or painful experiences. We will see ourselves with a deeper understanding as we examine our light and darkness in equal measure. We'll be reminded of hysterically funny and deeply painful events.

We are a culmination of all we have experienced, regardless of our perception, but we may have many misconceptions of ourselves. We must learn a way to see ourselves as we truly are, not through the projected perceptions of others. Our cellular self will take what it sees and hears as absolute truth, oftentimes swayed by hurtful words and reactions by others. Just because someone sees us through their perception, does not mean this is who we are.

Many of us as children were spoken to by others in a very cruel and demeaning fashion, leaving us with a lasting sense of diminished self-worth. As adults, those words haunt us in many aspects of our lives, and we have low self-esteem and very low confidence. But as adults we are responsible for ourselves and all that comes from us, and we cannot allow ourselves to be a victim of our childhood. The process of going within will bring much-needed emotional healing to the wounded inner child.

Much of our emotional imbalance in our adult life was created in our early childhood development, leaving our ego unable to evolve past this point, affecting us in great measure as adults. The journey inward allows us to have understanding of who we are and why, bringing a clear vision of what and how we need to change.

When we have understanding of why we have become who we are now, we can begin the healing process and further our Awakening Journey and evolution. We need to allow ourselves to go back through our lives to understand the events that bring our reactions and responses as adults.

Once we have an understanding of the "whys" in our lives, we can bring the changes we need to become our authentic selves, making navigation of our Awakening Process much easier. We had a saying at a factory I used to work at:" Work smarter, not harder." This is a great perception in many aspects of our lives to make our lives more simplistic. Bypass the unnecessary measures by refining and streamlining the many layers of many complex processes to navigate our Awakening Journey.

Just because the process may be complex, doesn't mean our lives should be. All too often, we look past the obvious, believing the answers to our questions are buried deep beneath a pile of useless rubble, and way too time consuming for our efforts. Start by peeling away the layers of complexity, throwing out what is not related to our main concern. Delete and file as necessary by asking if it truly matters or is a distraction. Trust your spirit self to know what needs to be sorted and discarded. Ask if it's ours or someone else's projection onto us, and toss what isn't ours.

Now, that we have determined our part in the equation, this is our focus. We will need to start looking for the root cause by going back through our lives with a microscope. We will find many related past experiences that will bring many memories, leaving us with a mixed bag of emotions. Don't get discouraged as these will sort themselves out as we go. Trust yourself in every aspect of your inward search by knowing your spirit will guide you every step of the way.

Our spirit always has our highest good in mind, so we must learn to trust that instinct speaking to us as we navigate our inward journey. Allow your 3D self to step back and trust the spirit. Give permission to the cellular self to let go of its perceived control, because it needs to know and accept that it is no longer in control, and the ego must give way for the heart-centered self to lead from now on. The inward journey is, in part, stepping away from the 3D and all of its limitations and constructs, toward the Higher Dimensions of the spirit within.

There will be an intense inner struggle as the mind and ego begin to let go of control, but you need to be diligent in your efforts with much self-discipline and self-trust. There is no time restriction as we are a constant work in progress, lasting beyond this lifetime. Don't feel it all must be done today. Remember, this is a process that takes however long it takes, not an event. When we feel the ego come to the front, don't give into its power. Sink back into the spirit self.

This is how we come to self-discipline and self-mastery, by not giving into old patterns and old beliefs projected onto us by others. You already feel the need to change and heal all of that, so simply allow it to happen. The uncomfortable feeling through this process is vulnerability and we must embrace this state, as it is where we grow spiritually and personally. Regardless of the level of comfort, push past the old ways of thought and change your mindset.

When you recognize the old patterns and beliefs, stop your thought process and integrate the new patterns and beliefs. Again, this is a process and not an event, so allow the process to work. Be compassionate and loving with yourself through these necessary changes. The cellular takes what we think and say as truth, so be mindful and aware of your thoughts and words toward the self. Never speak down to the self, but always give encouragement to bring confidence and positive change.

Focus on the perceived good of the self, but always have awareness of the perceived unwanted and unliked. We all know what we don't like in ourselves, and we should always strive to allow changes where needed, but we cannot focus on just that. Bring a balance within and give light to what we like about ourselves in equal measure. This will help us navigate through our sorting process as we find our own truths that are based in reality, not our perception of truth.

As we go within deeper, we will get to know and understand much about ourselves that we have chosen to forget for many reasons. This can and will bring extreme ranges of emotions, as we allow our emotional healing to proceed. Don't be alarmed with frustration or whatever your reaction and responses are. Allow your emotions to be heard by sitting within them and allowing them to exist. They have come to the forefront to be healed in layers.

You don't have to become your emotions, and they cannot be allowed to consume you, but you must allow yourself to feel them regardless of your emotional state. Again, be compassionate and loving toward yourself, always and in all ways. This emotional crisis is temporary, so keep this in mind. Tomorrow is another day and you'll make it through this day.

Chapter 8

Allowance

I speak often of allowance and allowing in regard to our Awakening Journey, as it is an integral part of our journey. This is a necessary mindset we all must trust and believe in, so we can assure that we evolve beyond our every today. This, for me, was very crucial in the early beginnings of my awareness of Awakening, and not a very easy change to make. Most of us are locked into what we believe we know to be truth. I'm now able to look back on my journey and see how I came to allowing myself to change my perception and my world.

I feel allowance is a most important step on our journey because it helps us to heal the wounded ego and inner child, enabling the changes we need to make within the spirit self. The cellular self is used to everything in our lives being a certain way and we have become comfortable within that. As we have more awareness of the self, we need to step out of our comfort zone and allow change.

Stepping out of our comfort zone brings us to that uncomfortable state of vulnerability, which is where we grow spiritually and personally. As we allow the spirit self to move toward authenticity, we can't help but change personally, so they go hand in hand, one moving the other. It is a beautiful balance of the 3D and spirit selves in the dance of evolution.

How do we allow and why is it necessary? We allow by simply changing our mindset from survival mode, victim mentality, and trying to control what we can't. All we have control of are our emotions, responses, reactions, thoughts, words, and actions, or in other words, what comes from us and not outer influences and environments.

We have been taught since we were babies that we must be in control of all we can be, all the time. We realize at some point on our journey that we are not in control of what is brought to us by the Universe. All of our experiences are meant to give us all we need to evolve, but the majority of us are led by the wounded ego and wounded inner child, which all too often bring a skewed perception, away from truth as it is.

To allow means to permit, which implies a lack of controlling, and a shift to letting come into existence and being. The mindset of allowing actually forces us to let go of the illusion of control, which is imperative to our journey. Changing our mindset is never easy as we are stepping outside of the comfort we have grown accustomed to, and permitting ourselves to be vulnerable, which many of us have been taught to perceive as weakness.

Contrary to common belief, the weakness is believing we are in control. It gives us a false sense of security by believing the truth we know is absolute and all else is not right. When we become immersed in what we believe as absolute truth, there is no room for expansion, and therefore no evolution. We become stuck in the status quo of our lives and we cannot move past that block. Openness to allowance is key to changing our mindset. It can and will bring the changes we need within.

We must take a step forward and upward, even if it is a small one, in order for there to be forward movement and evolution. Many of us have been taught, normally by ourselves, that we need to talk ourselves into change. If that works for you, then by all means, start convincing yourself. Regardless of how we change our mindset, just take that first step. Well, go on... take it. What are you waiting for? It all begins right here, right now. Take that step!

We can no longer put things off as we have done our entire lives, so change your mindset to begin immediately. Changing our mindset, once executed, will become a snowball effect as we see how easy it is, and we can begin to make numerous changes to the mind and the ways we used to do things. This is, in part, how we develop self-mastery, and when we have found our will, there can be no stopping us.

What am I talking about by allowing? There is no possible way to state all we need to allow, so I will give a few ideas and you can expand from here. One of the most important ways to allow is beginning with the self, where every change begins. If you need to speak out loud to give yourself permission then please do so, but give your cellular self permission to begin allowing changes to your mindset first.

Allowing the mindset change to happen is a noticeable shift within the self and you may feel that much dreaded "uncomfortable feeling" creeping in. This is change, and the cellular self does not like change and neither does the ego. Allow this feeling to exist, but keep telling the cellular self they are okay and be open to this. Change is never easy, but it doesn't have to be difficult.

Allowing ourselves to be the change we need will open us up to our will, which is so very important to making mindset changes. When we have found our will, we become an unstoppable force. I will discuss some obvious allowances necessary on our journey, and you can spread this out on your own once you have instilled this within the self. Again, change is difficult, but it doesn't have to be hard. Once we have implemented the proper mindset, we open ourselves to endless possibilities, realizing our authentic limitless self.

What are some possibilities we can look forward to? Again, it is an endless list, so we need to allow ourselves to be open to seeing the possibilities. It begins with permitting the self to begin seeing good and beauty, instead of focusing on the bad we have become accustomed to. We are all very adept at what we perceive to be failure, and all we are doing, in essence, is changing the old patterns and beliefs of focusing only on problems and not the solutions.

We can't possibly know how it feels to be successful until we feel "defeat." To quote the classic song "Dream On" by Aerosmith, "… You've got to lose to know how to win…" Giving the cellular self permission to begin seeing beauty instead of the ugly in our lives is a sure way to allowing beauty in our lives again. Our lives will undoubtedly become what we focus on. Instead of our focus being on our problems, begin to shift your focus to how it feels without those problems.

Many of us feel we have somehow found ourselves in a pit of despair, the rabbit hole, as it were, with no possible way out. The darkness we believe we need to endure is closing in around us, with no way to move beyond. I promise you, the only way to your light is through your darkness, but know this… you are the light in that darkness.

Go deep within, close your physical eyes, open your 3rd eye as much as you are able, and focus on your Sacred Space located near the Sacral Chakra just below your navel. This is the seat of your personal energy, some refer to as "prana" or "chi." No one can access this but you. This is a vast space we should think of as Our Holy Temple that contains the most sacred of the self—our energy.

Begin to allow energy to flow through this vastness. We can never force our energy, so we just allow it to flow. See your light even if it appears to be a small spark. Allow it to grow and it will, in time, fill this space meant only for you. This energy, although it can be used, can never be depleted. Around you is all the energy you will ever need and you have unlimited and constant access.

Allow this light to become brighter and allow it to expand, filling every cell in that general space. Perhaps you have a "feeling" as it grows within you, something akin to a full stomach after a good meal and maybe some "tingling" as well. This is you. This is your energy. Now allow this energy to flow to every cell in your body.

You can visualize this with your 3rd eye and possibly feel it coursing through your entire BEing. What does this have to do with allowing? I have stated many times everything begins with the self, what better way than to "feel" you in your most authentic state. What you are feeling is not just energy, it is love, our natural state of being.

Allow this to flow to every cell in your body, and you are feeling your own love, which is always present. The only way for this to change is if we allow that love to be overtaken by our darkness, a conscious decision that would derail our entire journey and purpose. But I ask you. How could you possibly allow this beautiful and amazing feeling to ever leave you?

You have just allowed yourself to feel within you what you have allowed to lay dormant by letting yourself get bogged down by the darkness you have been focusing on. Now look around you with your 3rd eye. Do you still see only darkness and no light? If so, then keep allowing. Not trying, allowing. Often our effort of trying is our block. It is not the outcome we focus upon, but the allowance to happen.

Keep focusing on that light, energy, and love as it flows throughout your BEing. When we allow ourselves to go one step further every day, then we are, in fact, assimilating and transmuting our cellular self. You'll find, eventually, that you have made it a way of life and it will just become something you no longer need to focus on. It will simply exist because you have allowed it to exist.

The character from Star Wars we all love and respect gave us some of the important lessons we could ever learn on our Awakening Journey. In specific, Yoda told the young Jedi Luke Skywalker, "...*Do or do not. There is no try...*". This, in effect, is saying, "Stop trying and simply allow." When we focus on trying, we can't be allowing because we are trying to control what is natural and organic. It is with trust and belief that we allow.

Yoda also stated, "...*You must unlearn what you have learned...*". This is a key point to our Awakening Journey as well, for indeed, we have been taught erroneously, so we must now learn truth and a corrected way of doing what we always have. This mindset of allowing ourselves to unlearn is going to change your life in more profound ways than you can imagine. Letting go of what we believed to be truth allows us to open to more than just possibilities, rather fact, truth, and probability.

Keep repeating this within yourself until it is a natural and unfocused flow. This is, in part, how we learn self-mastery and we can apply this principle to any aspect of our lives. There is always a process or procedure to accomplish all you need. There are no steps in concurrent measure, just however is best for you. This is your journey… live it your way.

Allow yourself to be authentic, not who you have been told you are. I realized around the age of 13 that I was not and could not be who my parents told me and expected me to be. It was too limiting and did not resonate with my spirit self in any way. This is normally one of the first signs of our Awakening Journey, to realize we can't be who we have been expected to be.

I express to many of my clients that we must be ourselves because everyone else is taken. Am I wrong? Each one of us are individuals on our own unique journey, and unique from all others. Not only do we need to allow authenticity, we must allow others to be who they are, and allow them their truth and their journey with respect.

None of us, not even within the parameters of a controlled experience, will experience the same event in the same manner. I often use the analogy of a speaker talking to a room of 150 people all being given the same message. There will be 150 different responses to that same speech, with their own interpretation of what the speaker said. Yes, there will be similar takes among their personal interpretations, but it carries a unique meaning to everyone present.

Respecting the journeys of others allows all of us to be uniquely different, as we cannot possibly fit into a model that society has deemed necessary we fit into. We have always been expected to fit into this nice little box given to us at birth and adhere to a common way of life. We, the Awakening, can no longer be limited to the confinements of any society. We are divergent, a part of all, and unlimited.

Allowing yourself to be you is quite an empowering thought. It gives us permission to be different. It does not, however, give us permission to believe we are better or in a higher place than others. We are never better or higher in status, nor are we beneath anyone else. We are simply unique, as our journeys are indigenous unto ourselves.

Not everyone on this planet is on an Awakening, spiritual, or healing journey and we must have allowance and respect that fact. Some may be young souls on a journey of discovery, some may be here to experience the very harshest of lessons and may have a life of extremes. Some have come here to experience a lavish and opulent journey, living a life many of us can only dream of.

These may not be our journeys, so we must accept and respect the journey of all others. It means their journey has nothing to do with ours and we certainly cannot compare ours to that of another. That is the proverbial task of comparing apples to oranges, an exercise in futility, and a meaningless endeavor. Wishing our life to be like theirs is a denial of our own truth, but we can make changes to our perception by accepting our journey as it is meant to be.

When we are unhappy within our journey, we need to ask the right questions in order to receive the right answers. *Why am I not happy?* Happiness is a daily choice we consciously make. Normally, we experience suffering because we cannot accept what is, and we resist what we cannot change. Resistance is futile. We always have three choices in any experience or situation.

Our first choice, can we change our current situation to the higher good of ourself and others. If we can, then we must act on the necessary changes. If we cannot, then we come to our second option. Can we change our perception of our situation and where we fit in for the betterment of our highest good? We need to carefully consider all aspects of our current state.

Changing our mindset and perception is a life changing challenge, but very necessary. Our ability to adapt, without compromising our integrity, can and will make our lives easier and better our position in life. The downside of not following our intuition and guides, is difficulty, and quite possibly, catastrophe. This is why we need to trust and believe in ourselves implicitly.

Once we have seen our position from as many angles as possible, we will determine that we either can or cannot change our perspective. If we can, then we implement the necessary changes within and create an internal environment we can succeed within. We have adapted and changed our life for the better.

Having made the decision that we simply cannot exist in any way, shape, or form where we stand within this situation, our third and most extreme decision is to walk away and look for other alternatives in our life. This decision can never be taken lightly and certainly not made from the ego. This decision has to be thoroughly thought through, exhausting all of our resources and with absolutely no other choice.

There will be times in our lives where the best-case scenario will be to quickly determine that moving on immediately is best for our higher good. We can only achieve our decisions through thorough discernment and diligence of sifting through all possibilities. Rash and quick decisions can and will sabotage our very existence, creating more trouble in the long run for ourselves.

Always… always make sure you have exhausted all your resources before coming to a final decision. Talking it through with someone wise and trustworthy is one way to ensure a successful outcome. Don't allow them to patronize you and simply say what they think you want to hear. Ask them to listen carefully and give only wisdom with options we may have not considered, as it is outside our scope of perception to see other options.

There will always be consequences to every decision we make, and sometimes we won't see them immediately. Sometimes we make a decision that isn't for our highest good, but how we respond, not react to this awareness will enable us to make changes in correcting an ill-fated decision. When it happens, and it will, always forgive yourself for not knowing better at the time.

Talking ourselves down and beating ourselves up for something we perceive as "stupid" or "dumb" of us, is self-defeating and can only bring us unnecessary guilt and shame, making life worse than it needs to be. Our cellular self listens to every thought and word, taking it as gospel truth. This old pattern only serves us to remain stuck in past habits that always bring us down and locked in place.

With awareness and recognition of any old pattern and belief, it can and will be changed, given the desire to change. Our Awakening Journey will always be about self-improvement, a never-ending process. We can either see ourselves as stupid or unworthy, or we can see an opportunity to learn, heal, and grow from what we have done. That is a conscious decision we all make.

Allowing ourselves to be a victim of the human condition, coming from a survival mentality, will make sure we won't evolve. Forgiving the self with love, compassion, and grace allows us to move forward, ensuring our evolution toward authenticity. This process is repeated time and again on our journey, but it doesn't mean we are moving backward.

Au contraire!!! We always move forward and upward regardless of our perception. Believing we are taking two steps forward, and one back, is incredibly self-defeating. It is impossible to move backward on our Awakening Journey, unless we insist on making sure we do through denial of our journey. This is a mindset change necessary on our journey.

Stepping out of the old patterns and beliefs is one way of ensuring our evolution and is done easily with the desire to move forward. That is the mindset change… having the desire to move forward instead of maintaining status quo. You possess the courage and strength to do whatever you put your mind to.

T.V. Evangelist Robert Schuller said, *"Don't just sit there… Do something!"* in a sermon many years ago. What he meant was that you must take an active role in your own life. The only way to get something done is to do it. Period. Don't live in fear anymore of what could go wrong. Change your perception to the opposite. Learn to trust and believe in yourself.

Choose to see what good will come out of it. Choose to see the beauty instead of the pain and suffering. Choose to see endless possibility instead of obstacles. Choose to live in love and not in fear. Choose to be free of the chains of limitation you've put around yourself. Choose to step outside of your comfort zone and embrace vulnerability. You will never evolve within the confines of the limits you have chosen.

Choose to live free. Choose to be the change you need. Choose to evolve and not remain stagnant. Choose what is for your highest good. Choose to always trust and believe in yourself. Choose to heal well and journey well. Choose to be authentically you. You have the ability... simply choose to allow yourself to... Do something good for you...

Chapter 9

Control

Ever since we were children, control has been a major part of our existence, whether we have been controlled or we are controlling. We have been controlled since birth, and now that we are aware of our Awakening Journey, we find ourselves needing to let go of controlling everything. Going back to our childhood to see patterns we have been taught in how to be masters of control, will bring the best possible start to letting go and transcend what we have been taught.

Every aspect of our lives was controlled by our guardians as babies, so right away we didn't have a choice in who we became. We can't place blame here because we were their responsibility and didn't have the ability to choose on our own. Our guardians did the best they could with what they had and knew at that time, so in being fair and just, we should forgive their efforts at this time. We were shown what they wanted us to see and were molded into their desire, and for some, made into smaller versions of our guardians.

Our very identity was given to us by what they believed, how they lived, what they considered right and wrong, political and religious views, even what we ate, was all just a reflection of their relationship with themselves. As we entered the education system, we were taught what they wanted us to learn, how to learn it, how we should act, how to dress, and even what was acceptable to say.

This continues throughout our whole existence, being made to fit into a societal system of hierarchy and class.

We never really had a chance to be our true selves because everyone felt they had to control us in all we became. Our religious beliefs and even our fundamental ethical and moral beliefs were forced upon us by every institution we came into contact with. No wonder we have trouble letting go of control in our lives when all we have been taught is that we have to be in control or be controlled. Now that we have awareness of our Awakening, our task is to undo all that has been done to and for us.

Our freethinking self, who knows we are limitless BEings, will need to start from the beginning to discover the old patterns and beliefs we need to overcome to allow our limitless self to take charge of our broken and shattered lives. How does one overcome lifetimes of being taught wrongful ways and ideology? We start by being aware of them.

When we have awareness, there is recognition, and when we have that recognition, we can begin to change our perceptions to transcending what no longer serves us. Every time we have recognition of an old pattern or belief, we can insert our own belief and pattern. It takes diligence and dedication to the self to even begin, but this is all about self-mastery and our Awakening Journey.

This is what's known as "going within" to make the changes that are necessary on our journey of evolution. Remember, there will be no evolution if we cannot transcend what we know and believe with trust. There is an old common belief that we are products of our childhood, but that does not free us from accountability.

We are indeed accountable for our thoughts, words, and actions, and we can no longer blame our childhood for who we are as adults. We have the ability to overcome and transcend all of this and we cannot use this as an excuse for how we are today. Own what is yours and accept it as a part of who you are, like it or not.

When we use our childhood as an excuse, we are playing the victim role and we're choosing to remain the victim. We are responsible for ourselves, so we can't blame someone else for who we are. It takes strength and courage to step out of the victim mentality and take responsibility for ourselves, which is essential to our journey.

So often we will say, "Well, nobody showed me the right way," or "Nobody taught me." That may be the truth, but you don't have to accept that as being the definitive way of life. Now that we are adults, it is up to us to learn what wasn't taught to us and unlearn what is no longer acceptable on our Awakening Journey.

Although who we are was forced upon us, we are intelligent BEings with the ability to discern right from wrong, even if we were not taught correctly. There are no longer acceptable excuses for not taking responsibility for our own actions, so it is up to us, and us alone, to make ourselves better than we were taught. This is a totally different time than our guardians lived in and many changes have come and gone. We have to be able to adapt to any and all changes and challenges we face. Many of these changes are within ourselves and those are the ones we have to keep in touch with, as change is the only constant on our Awakening Journey.

We are evolving, which means our truth is evolving as well. What we knew yesterday is not what we know today. Those stuck in 3D will see this as "changing our minds" and make it a bad thing, making us feel shame and guilt for not remaining static as they are. Accepting ourselves as limitless BEings is key to our freedom and transcending all that we were. We cannot allow the ways of others, or their needs, to keep us on their level to keep us from our evolution.

Peer pressure is not something we can give into, as it will only serve to keep us on a 3D level and keep us from our evolution. We cannot put any kind of importance upon the opinions of others because it really has nothing to do with our lives. They will try and project their viewpoints, forcing their truth on us in an attempt to justify their existence. We cannot give in to a 3D mentality any longer if we want to evolve.

Our Awakening Journey is about transcending 3D reality, evolving into a higher and limitless form of ourselves. It is a destructive process of unbecoming who we were taught to be and allowing our authentic self to surface and guide us. We have to let go of all control, all attachments, and all expectations of our lives in order to evolve.

There has to be implicit trust in ourselves, our journey, the process, and God to be able to surrender and allow life to happen. In our former 3D lives, we even tried to control God, bargaining for what we felt we needed. Spirituality would have us use man-made laws such as The Law of Attraction and The Law of Manifestation for materialistic gain.

By using positive affirmations, we put out to the Universe what we want and expect it to come to us because we "deserve it." What we are doing, in essence, is manipulating the Universe into giving us what makes us feel good in the form of material goods and money in our attempt to be happy. It is a manipulation of the process for our own 3D gain only. Our Awakening Journey is about our spirit, not the 3D body and its pleasures. Yes, bliss is our birthright as is abundance, but spirituality has us demanding our desires in the 3D, not spirit.

Our happiness, joy, and bliss will not come from materialistic gains, rather they are choices we make that come from within, not without. Our Awakening Journey is about our spirit, which does not need items to make us happy. We choose to be happy or not. If we truly need to feel good about something, then feel good about working toward healing the emotions and traumas of lifetimes and taking steps to further our evolution. That is where our happiness, joy, and bliss truly come from. They stem from the freedom of our self-mastery and healing ourselves of the pains that weigh us down from within.

Freedom is not found in owning objects, rather a state of BEing within our limitless authentic self. It is looking back at our 3D selves as we see our evolution, knowing we have overcome every obstacle we faced, and healing every pain and trauma we endured. Freedom is knowing that all the hard work we have done has made our spirit light in many different ways, knowing all the limits and constructs put in front of us are merely distractions.

The illusion that we control life was taught at an early age and awareness of our Awakening should bring us the understanding that we are not in control of life. Do you know it takes less energy to allow life to happen as it is meant to be, as opposed to trying to control it? That energy can be better used in doing all we need to ensure our evolution instead.

When we feel we must control our lives, our energy is focused outward in manipulating not only outcome but content. We think we need to have a plan for how we believe our life should be, which is often contrary to how it is meant to be. It only causes our energy to flow to an illusion we are creating within that comes from our wounded ego.

Trying to control our lives sets us into a fantasy concocted by the wounded ego, in an attempt to force our reality to fit some notion we knew in a childhood game, in an attempt to satisfy a need to make up for what we lacked as children. This "lack mentality" originates in early childhood development as we tried to reason what we wanted to make ourselves feel good.

Many of us, as children, were not given the proper nurturing we needed, often because we couldn't be seen as we were, but were seen through the perceptions of others, skewed by their own upbringing. The mentality of many of our guardians was, "It was good enough for me, so it's good enough for my children." This is a recipe for disaster in the making as many of us have found as adults.

We were raised for a time that no longer exists, by outdated methods, without thought for the individual being unique, using a "fast food" method of developing the masses in much the same way. The same parenting mold was used for generations. Now, as we enter the Age of Aquarius, ushering in the Divine Feminine, those aware of their Awakening have realized that this accepted socialization is no longer acceptable.

The age-old notion that children are to be seen and not heard is slowly being replaced with a need for the individual to be accepted as they are, and many of us are breaking the molds our ancestors embraced. Allowing ourselves to admit that their way is no longer acceptable is a major step in reforming how children are developing through more appropriate methods.

We, as adults, are bringing these reforms to mainstream idealism, and many of us are making the corrections within our adult selves and allowing healing to take place. The process of letting go of this ingrained illusion of control is coming to the forefront of those on their Awakening Journey.

How do I begin the process of letting go of this illusion of control? Once again, the awareness and recognition are in place and we must take action. The change the world needs can only happen within ourselves, so we must look within to see where we can make these internal changes. This process does not have to be hard or painful, so trust is necessary in allowing change.

We all contracted for the experiences in our lives to facilitate our evolution. Changing the mindset to accepting that we do not control these experiences can be a challenge, as any mindset changes we make. It is with sheer determination and understanding, with strength and courage, that we convince the wounded ego to allow these changes.

Letting go of control entails a certain level of healing the wounded ego and the inner child in order to change their perception. Give the cellular self permission to allow this change to the thought process. Accept the feeling of vulnerability as this is where we grow, and allow this process to be guided by your spirit self, not the ego.

Life becomes uncomfortable with the awareness of our Awakening Journey, but this doesn't mean it has to be hard or arduous. The "challenges" are a perception of the ego, as it has no desire to be pulled out of the comfort zone it has created for us to maintain a feeling of safety and familiarity. Our ego will tell us we have to fight the changes we need to make and will create distractions for us to make sure change does not come.

Change means work for the unhealed aspects of the self, so fears of the unknown will creep in. The ego is quite aware of how fear is an excellent source of control over the 3D self and its need to stay within our safety net. Now we need to make the choice between living in fear or allowing the self to evolve by living a heart-centered life of love.

Yes, living in fear is a choice we make every day. We have the same choice to live in love, coming from the heart-centered self with awareness. We don't have to absorb the energies and distractions of the outer world just because they exist. We make up our mind daily to choose the conscious decision to rise above the fears, face them head-on, and replace them with our own strength and determination to allow change.

This is one sure way in beginning our quest of letting go of believing we are in control. But I hear you asking, "Isn't this being controlling in itself?" Indeed!!! But now it's for the highest good of the self and not something to keep us from forward and upward movement. The difference is self-love and respect in allowing our evolution. This is, in part, the process of self-mastery, therefore necessary on our journey.

Learning to change our mindset is one of the greatest gifts we can give ourselves. It allows us to bring change in many areas of our daily lives. Change your perception, change your life. It may seem a little overwhelming to actually begin learning to change our mindset. That's the ego bringing fear to us... the distraction.

Learning to trust and believing in ourselves is one of our highest priorities to ensure our evolution. Again, this is also self-love and respect. We are, after all, unlimited BEings, so why shouldn't we allow ourselves to be? Give yourself permission to be a better version of your current self. You are deserving and most worthy of tapping into all of your untapped potentials.

Why can't I trust myself? For many of us, we've never given ourselves the chances we deserve. We've been taught to stay at a status quo and be happy with who we are and how we live. Since you're reading this, you're probably not happy and have a gnawing feeling that there is more than what you know. Ab-SOUL-utely there is, and once you make up your mind to allow it to be, you'll never be the same.

Changing the mindset begins with a need for change and followed through with determination and dedication. The more we want to change and are open to it, the more change will present itself to us through opportunities. Simply, speak to the Universe of your desire to embrace a new mindset, then act upon your intention.

It is hard work and you take your own pace. It's not a competition or race, and as long as we make an honest effort, it will happen. Intention is just another word unless there is action combined with it. You will only get out of any effort exactly what you put into it. If you put forth minimal effort, then you will receive minimal reward, so to speak.

Anyone who excels in their achievements has done so because they chose to take the extra step in order to push further and become better. I was repeatedly told as a child, "If you're going to do something, do it right and with the best of your ability." Wise words to follow and learn at a young age. It's never too late to learn.

As with any new endeavor we take, there will be times when we become frustrated, feeling as if we are taking two steps forward and one backward. This is the perception of the ego, who is not only demanding but incredibly whiny as well. Stop your thought process immediately when you feel this, breathe, and take some time for yourself. It's okay to honor what you feel, just understand why you're feeling it.

Talk to the ego as you would talk to another seeking help. Give it love and reassurance as you allow it to see a bigger picture of events and outcomes. Show it how life will be on the other side of your perceived issue. If you don't allow it to be a problem, then it won't be a problem. Remember as a child learning to ride your bike without training wheels?

There was an incredible drive to make it happen because we wanted to be able to enjoy the work we put into learning to ride the bike. We deserved to have fun. We were children and that's what we did. Well, that hasn't changed just because we got older, different, perhaps, for different reasons, but we're still deserving of enjoying the fruits of our labor. Why else would we try new things?

It is not possible for backward movement in a progressive state. What is happening, in actuality, is that we stay where we are temporarily, whether to just rest for a bit, rejuvenate, or allow an aspect of our healing to catch up. I promise you, you're not going backward, so stop believing you are and soon you'll feel that forward movement.

That's a change in mindset, to change the old belief that we're taking backward steps, to that of it being temporary and actually a good thing happening within our process. There is so much going on within us that we are not aware of and all of it has purpose beyond our scope of awareness. This is why we must trust.

TRUST yourself, TRUST your journey, TRUST the process, and TRUST God. This is an incredibly necessary mindset to make for ourselves at any time for any reason. Without trust, there is no evolution. Not blind trust, but with discernment that we're listening to our spirit self and not the other inner dialogue of the ego or the wounded child. Knowing your own energy is the only way to discern the difference.

This is also, in part, self-mastery, knowing yourself on deeper levels as your evolution takes place. This is also the journey within, of Awakening, the journey you're on as you read this. The openness to change can and will bring change itself, and the allowance of change will ensure its continuity.

Change will never happen for us until we're ready for it, so please be patient with yourself as this process takes form. We can't force it, so allow it to cultivate and happen organically. Be loving and nurturing with the self through this process, as life will be complicated at times. Always remember this: You're always exactly where you're meant to be on your journey.

Allow change to happen as it's meant to, not how you believe it should be. By all means, dedicate to it with strong determination. Find your inner courage, and you'll find the will and conviction needed for your journey to progress and evolve. Keep breathing, especially when the frustration sets in, because it will from time to time.

Never look ahead and tell yourself how far you have to go. Be aware of this, but never focus on it, as it only serves to sabotage our journey and our efforts. Always look back long enough to see how far you've come, but don't stay long and don't gloat about your achievements. See them with grace and humility, while still celebrating your hard work.

We will spend our lives finding balance in every aspect, so remember we are a work in progress, and perfection is subjective. We are perfectly imperfect as we are. That means, for today, we are as perfect as we can be, as long as we have done something to better ourself. The Universe isn't perfect, so why should we believe we're better than the Universe, having the ability to achieve perfection? We are much better off humble, rather than arrogant and foolish.

Chapter 10

Change

Change is the only constant on your Awakening Journey. As we evolve toward our authentic self, we are in a state of constant change. This growth we experience is also bringing a change in our truth. It is necessary to have awareness of the self in all aspects to be able to keep up with the many changes of our growth. Some changes will be subtle and hardly noticeable, while others will be quantum, often becoming uncomfortable. This is a state of vulnerability as we are stepping outside of the comfort zone we have created for ourselves.

Throughout our entire life, we have made a comfortable nest to exist within, maintaining a feel-good state, enabling ourselves to live without much growth. This status quo is a major block on our Awakening evolution, as there is no room for expansion. In order to allow our evolution, we must give ourselves permission to let go of all we believe and what we thought was our truth.

Beginning at birth, our lives are not our own and we have already lost our identity. Every institution we were supposed to trust, is shaping us into a conformity of someone else's reality and truth, beginning with the family unit. Our chosen guardians instilled in us their truth and how they believed we should be nurtured, taking us away from our authentic self. We were exposed to many different beliefs, being taught what to think, how to act, what to believe, and who we were expected to become.

When our guardians help us develop into balanced beings, we will be able to live a life filled with many beautiful and wonderful things. The flip side is that we find a life of struggle as we were not shown how to properly navigate this lifetime. When we have become aware of our own spirituality, we begin to see the truths instilled within us that need to change. Some realize the momentous task ahead and will face it with grace, while others will not know how to begin this process of change. So, how do we understand how to be the change we need?

Begin with accepting the need for change, and bring awareness to the wounded ego, taking charge of what we can within our journey: Our thoughts, words, actions, reactions, and responses. We will always have free will, but we also have purpose within our existence, and when we have awareness of our Awakening Journey, we recognize the need to follow our Divine Path. Unfortunately, most of us have never been shown how to step away from who we were and into who we truly are.

This guide is written from an Awakening perspective, meant to bring knowledge of navigating your Awakening Journey from a deep spiritual wisdom. I have stated often that everything begins with awareness. If we have no awareness of a different way than what we know, there will be no evolution of the self or our journey.

This is a good beginning, and now we can set the intention to act upon our awareness, and we must take the first step toward the change we need to be.

What is the first step and how do we make it? We have already spoken our intention, now we simply put action to our intention. I was already deep into my journey when the New Age movement came into existence in the late 1970s with Positive Mental Awareness. I was a sponge, absorbing all I could about their version of spirituality, but I couldn't help feeling that there was way more to this than what we were told.

It was a good foundation but was incredibly limited to very superficial ideals. I took from it one of my personal foundations with this one simple thought: Every day we reinvent who we are. Every day we have an opportunity to become closer to our authentic self. I knew at this point I would be a constant work in progress until my final breath in this existence. I was ready to embrace my journey and become my authentic self.

I would begin my day with gratitude for yet another opportunity to be more than who I was. I had acceptance of my need to change and allowed myself to do whatever was necessary. I knew it was going to be a difficult journey, so rather than perceive it as an arduous task, I looked at it as an adventure, accepting the challenges and experiences along the way. I've had many challenges and I embraced them all, facing them head on, and all the fears that come with those challenges.

The process of change has many different layers and levels, and each one must be taken in stride and accepted as a part of our journey, otherwise we end up with much trauma and unnecessary struggles. Change can be difficult to navigate, but there are broad measures we can take to assist us through these uncomfortable times. You'll have many experiences meant to propel you into the change needed for your evolution. Some we will perceive as good, some bad, some beautiful, and some horrific.

The experience is neutral, neither good nor bad. It is our perception that brings definition to any experience. We always have the choice to allow ourselves to be a victim or see opportunity to learn, heal, and grow. We often take a single experience and gauge the rest of our lives on that single experience, believing it to be an absolute truth of measure. I see this often in others who are seeking a spiritual experience. First off, we must know we will be brought new experiences necessary for our evolution.

I cannot stress enough the need for trust on our journey. I have told every one of my clients this one simple thought that I feel helps us all as we evolve: Trust yourself, trust your journey, trust the process, and trust God. When we are able to put this all together, we are ready to let go of the illusion that we are in control of our lives. Our journey and all that it encompasses was contracted before we incarnated into this lifetime. When we trust, we allow our journey and our Divine Purpose to be what it is meant to be, not what we think it should be.

When we allow our life to be what it is meant to be, we bypass the wounded ego who believes things should be a certain way, and our perceived control gives way to allowance of our higher truth. Again, we are changing, and our truth must change as well. Who we were yesterday, and often several minutes ago is not who we are now, and the same goes for our every tomorrow. Accept what is inevitable and choose the mindset you need for your evolution.

Once we have chosen the mindset of allowance, the only one capable of stopping us is ourselves. Life is a mindset and how we react is going to set in motion all that follows. This is our free will, so we need to be quite attentive to how we react and respond to any given situation and experience. Learning to allow our perception to change is key to our growth, personally and spiritually. The mindset of accepting that we are not in control will facilitate an improved perception, allowing any truth given to be as it is meant to be, and not what our ego perceives it to be.

Now that we can begin to allow change for this new mindset, we can give ourselves permission to be open to receiving any change on our journey. The willingness and openness to change, can and will bring change itself. That's one of the new mindsets we need to embrace as Awakening BEings to ensure our evolution.

Openness brings availability of expansion. Expansion brings evolution. Evolution ensures we become our authentic self, the spirit.

Oftentimes, we must give the cellular self permission because it does not have awareness beyond what it knows. We must also be careful as to how we speak to the self, and think, as the cellular tends to take our thoughts and words as gospel truth. Speak and think kindly to the self with compassion, love, and grace, nurturing the wounded child and ego that are normally in control. Let the physical body know it is okay to allow the changes coming, and to cooperate with the heart-centered self that is bringing the change we need. This heart-centered self is our spirit, and this is where our authentic self resides.

Our spirit will always guide us on our journey, making sure we follow according to our purpose, so we need to pay close attention when it speaks. I learned many years ago we must be best friends with our Higher Self and allow them to be our guide. We have the ability to close our ears and eyes and to hear and see from the heart via the 3rd Eye. This is located in the center of the forehead, above the eyes, and is connected to the pineal gland. This is where our gifts are, and we need to allow ourselves to be accustomed to using the 3rd Eye instead of our eyes and ears.

When we can do this effectively, we will begin to realize truth as it is meant to be, not how our wounded ego wants us to perceive it. This process is a major and necessary change on our Awakening Journey. All we need is already within us, and we must learn to stop relying on our 3D self to be our guide. The Awakening Journey is, in part, walking away from the constructs and limitations of the 3D, and inward toward the Higher Dimensions, which are within us.

We must also stop seeing ourselves as a body and allow the true perception that we are spirits having a human experience. This will go a very long way to bringing the trust we need so badly on this journey. We are not defined by the body we inhabit, but by the spirit, our authentic self. Allowing these changes in mindset will facilitate allowance for many of the processes we will undertake on our evolution.

I have another saying among many: Change your perception, change your life and your world. When we allow ourselves to see things from a new and different angle, we will inevitably see a different reality. We are the co-creators of our personal world, not the outer world, but we can change the outer world by seeing things from a different perspective. Learning to be the observer allows us to experience without judgment.

Allowing the self to experience without judgment affords us the ability to realize truth as it is meant to be, not as our wounded ego wants us to perceive it. The ego is really good at showing us what it wants us to see, not necessarily what is real and true, drawing from experiences it has determined to be other than truth. The ego is not a bad thing within us that needs to be destroyed or done away with, contrary to common belief within many spiritual mythologies.

When the ego is healed and balanced, it becomes our will and determination, with such strength that nothing can stop it from carrying out our Divine Purpose. The healed and balanced ego is one of the greatest assets we possess, and it will propel us to quantum leaps on our journey. It is a part of the self, undeniably, and in part, a very necessary aspect of our entire BEing.

Changing our perception to the need for the ego to be balanced and healed is a change we must make early in our Awakening development. Awareness of the ego and its responses and reactions will bring a myriad of necessary changes without even trying. Keeping our lives simple and uncomplicated is also a change we must make early in our awareness of the self. The many processes within our journey are complicated, but we don't have to allow our lives to be complicated.

Keeping simplicity within our lives brings more openness on the many levels and layers of our journey. The simple, yet necessary change in perception of allowing life to be what it is meant to be, and not what we think or believe it should be, is huge for our journey. Allowing others to be who they are and not as we need them to be, will again bring many changes without effort.

We can't expect others to be like us because we are all on very different journeys, with very different purposes, and we are all at different points on our perceived journeys. Not everyone will be able to see our perspective because they haven't experienced what we have, and certainly not how we have. When there is no expectation in our lives, there can be no disappointment, which comes from others or ourselves not living up to them.

Learning to let go of expectations is incredibly liberating. We are letting go of a perceived control and learning to allow what is, which brings a breath of freedom. It actually takes less energy to allow than it does to control. *Wait. What?* When we don't feel the need to control, our energy is focused on us and not on what we are trying to control. I had to think about that realization long and hard.

Letting go of expectations and attachments of how we believe our lives should be is how we begin to let go of the illusion that we are in control of our lives. It simplifies our lives as it affords us the opportunity to focus inward and away from external distractions meant to drag us away from our Divine Purpose. Having attachment means we either have ownership, or are owned by ideals, objects, and people, which we don't, and aren't. We are sovereign BEings not owned by anyone or anything, especially all that is from the 3D and our past.

Letting go of the illusion of control brings us back into the moment from looking too far into the future. This moment is all that is real, as the past no longer exists and the future is yet to be. Living in the present allows us to accept what life is meant to bring us for our evolution. We also must remember everything happens as it is meant to, when it is meant to, or what we refer to as "Divine Timing", and not our belief of when and how it is meant to be.

It truly does take less of our energy when we know and accept that we are only in control of what comes from us, because all we need to do is either respond or react to any given situation. Accept what is, and focus on how to properly respond and react from the heart, not the ego. This awareness is in part self-mastery and will ensure our evolution. This alone will bring many changes in old patterns and beliefs, allowing us to step away from any 3D concept, and into our authentic self.

This new belief will also support us on our emotional healing journey, bringing an openness and liberation from the chains of oppression brought to us from early childhood development. Healing the wounded inner child is nothing more than healing and balancing the wounded ego. Many of our egos never evolved past our grade school years and this is problematic in how we react to current experiences.

The ego will usually respond with a negative commentary, bringing us into survival or victim mode. Our response and reaction must be from the heart and away from past traumas that lead us further into survival or victim mentality. This will take much unnecessary pressure from ourselves. Learning to see an opportunity to learn, heal, and grow, instead of asking "why" will further take us out of a self-sabotaging mindset, with an openness to allowance and acceptance of truth.

Changing old patterns and beliefs is a relatively simple process, again, beginning with awareness of them. As we begin to recognize an old pattern or belief, we need to stop our thought process immediately and interject the new belief and pattern. It is a process and will take time, not an event that brings change immediately. We must allow patience in any process to fully come around to the change we need.

Again, don't be afraid to give the self permission for any change to come, as the cellular self will stroll along the same path it always has. Be steadfast in your awareness and efforts through any process of change. It takes determination, perseverance, and dedication to anything we want to be successful in. Michael Jordan didn't become a basketball legend without constant and diligent work at his craft, and neither will you. Make the change in your mindset to do what is necessary.

We are only going to receive from life what we put into it. If you have always done "just enough to get by with" then expect mediocrity and status quo. The moment we go above and beyond in any measure, we ensure forward movement. Drive yourself to be somehow more or better than the you of yesterday, and in a short time you will begin to see your own evolution, even through difficult times.

How quickly you evolve will be determined by your willingness and effort, with the understanding we are not in competition with anyone or anything. There is no time limit, and no set date for our journey to be all it is meant to be, so don't pressure yourself to be an overachiever, missing out on lessons we need to learn. Learn to pace yourself, but still be driven without making it a sprint to a perceived finish line, because there is none.

Stop to take time for you to replenish what needs to be refueled. Take "downtime" as you need, time for yourself. Your mental and physical health is something you need to be aware of. Allow yourself to relearn how to see the beauty in life, focusing on the better aspects in all you experience. Remember, what we focus on is what our lives become.

Chapter 11

Process

Our whole existence is based upon a series of processes. From the time we wake up to the time we go to bed, our day is one process after another with some overlapping. So, why is it necessary to even discuss what is obvious? We need to understand process to bring a whole new awareness not only to our daily life, but ourself as well. From an Awakening viewpoint, it is a series of processes, and we need to have deeper understanding of how this actually fits into our journey.

So many of us, myself included, were expecting events to take place to mark our progress on our Awakening Journey. Yes, there will be events that take place, but our journey is one long process, normally extending from lifetime to lifetime. Sometimes it can seem pretty meaningless to be engaged in a process that probably won't be completed before we cross over to being our Light-Self again.

Really, what's the point? As stated earlier, we need to have awareness of our processes to bring a different and deeper understanding of ourself through our Awakening Journey. The inward journey of Awakening is in part, self-mastery, getting to know ourselves with an ever-deepening understanding. The more we know ourself, the more understanding we have of why we do what we do and who we are.

Our day will always start with waking from, hopefully, a good night's rest. We stretch a little, bringing movement back into the body and blood flow that was lacking as we slept. We clear the sleep from our eyes, yawn, rub our face, and stretch some more. Perhaps we had to turn off the alarm clock before we did any of this.

As we come back to life, we throw the covers off our body and drag ourselves to the bathroom and enjoy that first morning constitutional function. We then wash our hands, return to the bedroom, and attempt to adorn ourself with some kind of clothing as has become our morning ritual, while still attempting to allow our brain to function. Like many, we make our way to the kitchen and proceed to make the nectar of the gods known as coffee.

Some of us may turn on the TV, some of us turn on our computer or phone, and some of us will just sit, still trying to clear our heads enough to start our day. But our day has already started! Many of us are not aware of the morning rituals we have become accustomed to and have become comfortable within, as we have found something that works for us. Many of us give no thought to our morning routine as we are still trying to awaken.

Oh, awaken. It's much the same for us in the morning as when we begin to have awareness of our Awakening Journey. We know something is different as we begin to climb out of the fog of our slumber, but the necessary awareness has not been presented as of yet to us. See where I'm going with this? In order to know where to begin, we have to understand what it is we're doing.

Without awareness there can be no understanding. As we live our journey, we begin to have recognition of how we utilize simple processes to evolve. When we have recognition, we have acceptance. Now we begin to realize the self on a different level. This is how self-mastery works, through the realization of the self. If we don't recognize the self, we cannot evolve on the Divine Path set before us.

So, where am I taking this to? Knowing ourselves with deeper understanding brings to light a fresh sense of who we are and why we do the things we do. This is self-mastery in progress. As I have stated many times before, I will state many more times: the more we know and understand about ourselves, the clearer our understanding of our evolution.

Everything on our journey is a process: Healing, our gifts, knowledge, wisdom, and proper use of them are all process. Let's begin with the process of healing emotional traumas, as it's essential to our Awakening Journey. I really can't stress enough how important this is. We've spent lifetimes avoiding what we must do, and those of us on healing journeys need to know this well.

Emotional healing is not pushing our traumas down and forgetting about them. This is exactly why we're in the spot we're in, as we have done this for lifetimes. As with everything, there is awareness that normally begins with a trigger response. *Why did I get triggered?* Because, sunshine, we've managed to continually ignore the reasons why.

It all began somewhere in our early childhood development as a trauma. Perhaps we were rejected, shunned, made to feel guilty, even got into trouble and didn't fully understand what we did. Regardless, that memory keeps coming up at the most inopportune time, and yet we continue to ignore it. To begin the healing process, stop ignoring it and allow it to present itself, and allow it to exist.

Some type of experience just brought a trigger response. A trigger response occurs when we experience a familiar feeling brought on by a sudden memory, an event, or experience. Perhaps someone says or does something that will bring an emotional response, giving us a sense of feeling uncomfortable, possibly anger, and we don't know why.

However we feel this response, we must allow it to exist. The emotional healing process can now begin with recognition and acceptance of it. This will take some deep inward effort as we begin to trace back through our life to find similar experiences with similar feelings. We somehow are able to keep track of these experiences, which enables us to put them all together to find the common grounds.

We're basically building a filing system in one of our brains, either cranial, heart, or stomach. Now we can look at the files to see similarities. Through the process of collating this data, we begin to see a picture of these similarities. This brings us an understanding of possibilities. Sometimes it will take much time, even lifetimes, to reach the root issue before we can actually heal the trauma.

Don't get discouraged and upset with yourself when frustration sets in. Be loving and compassionate. This is a process that takes time, not an event, therefore, it can be drawn out and quite extensive. Breathe. This is quite necessary to our journey, so trust the process and allow it to work.

As we are gathering our information, we will begin to see a spiderweb start to form with many more files adding to our database. This is a very good thing because it shows us that our efforts are beginning to pay off. The more we're able to recognize, the more we're able to heal. We will see at some point that we're actually healing multiple issues simultaneously.

This shows us without a shadow of doubt that we are being quite successful in allowing the process to work. This is not something we really need to think about constantly on a conscious level. As with anything else, the rate at which we learn becomes quicker and easier with repetition and expansion. Doing something often certainly makes us better at our task, eventually being able to do it without much effort. Remember always, we're limitless BEings and allowing processes to be successful opens us up to more opportunities.

Eventually, we should be able to connect all the dots and our picture becomes more clear and quite larger in size. We're able to simply grab a file that is relative to a current experience, sort through it, and begin the healing process. As we look back upon these experiences, we need to see them from a different perspective in order to see truth.

How do we see from a different perspective and what does it mean? Seeing from a different perspective simply means not through our own physical eyes and emotional self. That is the memory, and perhaps not the truth as it happened. Oftentimes our perception is being led by the wounded ego, who is unable to see beyond itself.

To be able to see from a different perspective, we must learn to step outside of our 3D self and into the spirit self. Our spirit sees only truth from a higher place of existence, and not from the physical plane. Our connection with our spirit self is incredibly essential to our evolution, with absolute trust and belief. They define who we are, not the 3D self.

For those of us who don't know how to achieve this, and I absolutely do remember not knowing, start with this exercise and modify it to what works for you, as this is merely a guideline that worked for me personally. It's really just a form of meditation and the process of going within.

Always begin with relaxing the body, taking deep breaths to release tensions, allowing the whole self to relax. Allow yourself to slip into a state of mindlessness by focusing on either the Christ Conscious center where your rib plate comes together, or your Sacred Space near your Sacral Chakra.

Relax your muscles from the top of your head slowly down through your body while breathing normally, releasing tension and stress. Ask your spirit self to come forward and guide you inward with acceptance of their presence. Allow the mind to clear the mental clutter, feeling your spirit self come into being. Relax the physical body further until you feel calm. Take normal breaths.

At some point here, we may begin to feel a new energy presence. This is the spirit coming forward as we have asked. Allow this to overtake your very existence, and become one with this energy which is your authentic self. You may begin to feel an overwhelming sense of love filling every cell in your physical body.

This is who you are authentically. Some of us may feel a deep desire to cry while others may feel nothing. Both are okay. Don't feel discouraged if you don't feel a difference, as some of us will need more time to allow the spirit self to become present. It's all a part of the process. Allow it to work organically, not how we want it to.

Once we feel the spirit fill our entire BEing, allow the silenced mind to call forth the memory we have chosen to revisit. Allow it to come into our 3rd Eye view, but stand to the side and see it through your spirit self, not with your physical eyes. Observe the memory as an outsider and watch it unfold.

You have now stepped outside of the ego's perception of judgement if you truly allowed the spirit self to lead you. Now play the memory again with emotional detachment and see the truth of the experience. It took me some time to learn how to allow the spirit to see for me. It's a process and takes time to learn, so allow it to be organic with patience.

Once the memory comes to light and we have no emotional ties to it, we can begin to see it as it really happened, not as we perceived it. Make mental notes as to the differences between our emotional attachment and truth through the spirit self. Allow it to play as many times as is necessary to see the differences.

This is, again, us learning to let go of the egos perception to see the truth. Many times, I have revisited a memory that brought a trigger and have been able to see it really didn't happen as I believed. I saw myself in a different reality of truth from a higher perspective, with the realization of my vision and memory to be totally wrong.

So many times, I have seen myself take something how my ego chose to take it and not as it was intended. The hard part here is being able to admit to the self with acceptance of our error of perception. It's not always easy to admit to the self that we were wrong. The ego doesn't like to be told it was wrong.

This is how we heal and balance the ego, as well as see truth to be able to allow the process of emotional healing from a higher perspective. Once we have seen the truth, we must accept it, and forgive ourselves with love and compassion. Many times, I have called the spirit of all others involved to make my apology and ask forgiveness.

I have used this mantra for many years to make amends for my misperceptions:" I forgive those who may or may not have done me harm and ask forgiveness from those I may or may not have brought harm to." Please feel free to adapt this to a form that works for you. Again, I bring you suggestions and guidelines. Please find what works for you.

Once we have seen truth, allow yourself to come back to the present, asking the spirit self to remain in place. Having the awareness and recognition of our spirit energy will help us maintain their presence and rightful place as our guide. Once again, we are not defined by the 3D, rather the spirit self.

These are just examples to be used throughout your journey inward, and can be useful in many other areas of even our daily lives. As with any task we undertake, we become better with more use, and it does become easier each time we use it. Everything I have brought to your attention has worked for me, so please adapt it to your need.

Using and understanding the many processes described will enable us to change old patterns and beliefs, bringing the necessary shifts within our journey. This is a way of life and not just a technique or concept. I truly live my life in this fashion as it has become second nature to me. This is the journey of self-mastery in progress.

Adapt these processes to fit your way of life and incorporate even the most subtle of changes in creating your version. Allow what is meant to be, not how we perceive it to be. Always and in all ways trust and believe in yourself. Allow the spirit self to guide you, not the ego. Change is never easy, but it doesn't have to be difficult.

I pray you're beginning to see how we live by a series of processes, and are starting to have a deeper sense of yourself. For those of us having difficulty or struggling to understand, please don't despair and become frustrated. Keep being gentle and compassionate with yourself. Process takes time to work. We can't see them as events as we have come to expect some quick fix.

We didn't become the way we are overnight, so don't expect change to happen right away. With persistence in our efforts, we can achieve a dream come true, and realize how much more we are than what we believe. This is how we begin to see our untapped potential and become the limitless BEings we truly are.

Please don't see this as a task to undertake, as this makes us feel as though we have to accomplish it as soon as we can. Allowing time to learn, heal, and grow takes any internal pressure off of us. We can't be disappointed if we have no expectations. Let go of any attachments as well, as this brings some type of ownership. Allow it to be organic, as it's meant to be.

...Let go of how you believe your life should be.
Allow what is meant to be...

Chapter 12

Knowing Our Value

We all can trace back to our childhood when others have projected their need onto us to make us feel less than who we were. As children, we have not developed the ability to not take all we were told as truth and believe it as truth. It all started within our families, school, church, society, and even ourselves.

We didn't have the understanding that what was projected onto us didn't have anything to do with us, so we took it personally and ended up feeling guilt and shame, disliking ourselves. We didn't know any better about ourselves, and we took those words as truth, and they became our identity.

I remember hearing repeatedly from a beloved adult, "You will never amount to anything and will always be a piece of shit." As a child, when we are repeatedly told something, it doesn't take long before we take it as our truth, and we become exactly what we are told. Unfortunately, many of us never heal words as damaging as these, and the wounds never heal.

That was incredibly painful to hear then and it took me till I was 50 years old to realize I was not what I was made to believe. I am, in fact, quite proud of what I have achieved and who I have become. I gave forgiveness every time I heard those words or the memory came up. Some wounds will take years, possibly lifetimes, to fully heal.

We all were bullied as children, which added to our feeling less than who we are and worth. Children can be incredibly mean and vicious when they feel they need to make themselves appear bigger and better than those they perceive as weak. They will prey on any they deem weaker in stature, character, or even social class. I remember many kids in grade school making fun of others simply because they were poor, not understanding it was not a choice.

All too often, children with learning disabilities come from families that are not as well-educated as others. Societal class idealism is passed onto children, often with upper class children thinking they are better than those of the middle and lower classes. This has always been, and they believe themselves to be privileged. Unfortunately, society shows them favor in many ways over other children more capable, strictly based on the family name and perceived social caste.

Many times, a bully is developed because their home life is abusive and neglectful. These children act out their frustrations onto others in an attempt to feel good about who they are, as they don't receive positive reinforcement at home. These children are usually labeled troublemakers and end up having difficult lives, never being able to heal their pains and traumas.

Our prison systems are full of them, and others are taught to be as they are by their guardians and families. Society shuns and discards them because it is believed they will never be able to rehabilitate and heal, and they are never given a chance to be otherwise. Another unfortunate truth is society doesn't care about them either, and they continue being pushed aside.

We never know what others are going through, yet, again, society doesn't have the time or the inclination to truly look into the lives of others. They are seen as other than acceptable and they are forgotten about. Many who fall into a trap of violence don't realize there are other choices, because no one ever cared to help them. It's the old adage, "evil you see, evil I am." They don't have the ability to see beyond what they know, and unfortunately, remain trapped within their truth as it has been projected onto them.

Those older than us, either didn't care or didn't understand how impressionable children are. Children are like sponges, absorbing and retaining all information they come in contact with, without discernment or the ability to discard bad information. They will take what they hear and learn as truth, and it will remain until new information comes in and replaces those truths. As adults, we are much the same, but we have the ability to reject what doesn't resonate, or just don't believe.

The whole time a child absorbs information, they are becoming aware of their own identity, and are discovering and experiencing life through their own point of view. They still need to be shown truth, but now they are developing a thought process and are able to begin sifting through information, but still able to accept all as truth. Everyone who comes in contact with a child will attempt to project their beliefs at some point, leaving the child confused about reality, not knowing what to believe. They depend on the family unit, as those they trust, to bring them points of reference they will determine as truth.

A child's early years are filled with information aimed at their development, to fit within what society deems as being acceptable, without understanding that all children develop at different rates and ways. We end up with generations of children being brought up to live in a time that no longer exists, with outdated concepts and ideas, eventually raising yet another generation of BEings just as messed up as the last. No wonder so many grow into adulthood not being able to cope with reality, and a society that doesn't understand them.

We end up with medical misdiagnoses, brilliant spirits believed to be less than acceptable by societal standards. The individual needs have never been accepted by society, and it is believed if one is different, they are flawed. I personally was a gifted child in many ways, was stifled, told I was wrong, and made to believe there was something wrong with me.

My self-esteem tanked, I didn't like myself, and was shunned because I was different. Like many of you, I never felt like I belonged in my family or society, so I isolated myself from both in an attempt to hide from the world. Today, I still don't feel as though I fit in, but I have accepted myself unconditionally, without the need to hide my authentic self.

Take yourself back to your childhood, yes, relive the harshness and trauma, because somewhere back there, your inner child hid when you fragmented, leaving you with just a part of your whole BEing. I ended up just not caring anymore, because whatever I did wasn't good enough for the expectations put on me by family and society.

I acted out because I didn't know how to express myself, and was labeled a troublemaker. No child truly knows how to express themselves, and eventually all those bottled-up emotions will come to the surface, normally in an explosion, only to end up being punished, not knowing exactly why.

Many of our parents and caretakers treated us the way they were treated by their parents because they simply didn't know that there was another way. Many of us growing up in the '50s through the '70s had parents that were brought up during a time of war, so they had to learn survival skills.

Yes, we had Vietnam, but we also were brought into the dawning of the Aquarian Age, and suddenly, it became vital to the youth and young adults to step out of what we were taught. It wasn't enough for them to just simply survive, and love became an issue, because many of our parents had become emotionally barren and had forgotten how to be love. We knew we were loved, but we didn't understand why we were punished so heavily for being ourselves, for being a child.

A society of young people came together as a whole and started a revolution against the system because they knew their worth and value. Our society and a flawed system needed changed. We are still fighting this very system today because it is still being run by those brought up in a time that no longer exists.

This progression of evolution is being thwarted, despite our efforts to bring awareness and attention to the fact that love is lacking in our world. All of us on an Awakening Journey, whether we realize or not, are in the process of bringing change to our world.

Why is this change necessary? Simply, the Aquarian Age is bringing the balance of the Divine Feminine and Masculine energies to the forefront, and we can no longer tolerate the status quo that has been in place for thousands of years. We have a much different understanding and outlook on life because of our Awakening.

We see how important the individual is, even if we are all a part of the Oneness, the Stream of Consciousness. Yes, we are all from the same Source, but on our own personal journey aimed at healing the Oneness. We can only bring healing by healing ourselves, bringing change to ourselves, changing the world, one BEing at a time.

Through self-awareness, we must know our worth and value, if only to the self. How do I find my own worth and value? We find it by going within. We find it by trusting ourselves and believing in ourselves, even if no one else does. We don't need validation or acceptance from anyone outside of ourselves.

I'm constantly saying to others that how other people view us or feel about us has nothing to do with us. How they see and feel about us is a reflection of their relationship with themselves, and we cannot take it personally. Their opinion of us is really none of our business, and has no effect on us, unless we allow it to. No one can hurt us without our permission.

I used to truly care what others thought about me because I was raised to be a people pleaser and to believe I was much less than I am, like many of us. We are taught from birth who we are. Times have changed because we are changing, as a society, stemming from energies coming at us from the cosmos. We simply cannot afford to put others first as we were taught.

Be aware of others, yes, but we must live our lives for us because it is our life. They projected onto us our whole life, and it never settled well with many of us because we just knew it was wrong. We came to this life with that understanding and knowing. We don't have to know why we know it; we just have to accept that we know it.

We have to have recognition and awareness of these old patterns and beliefs in order to bring the change within ourselves needed to know our worth. We must live our lives as we see fit, without bringing harm to anyone, including ourselves. We can no longer allow others to live their failures vicariously through us, bringing them the healing they need. We are our number one priority and focus, and it is not selfish to be true to ourselves.

We must understand that no one can help us, or take care of us as we need, so it is up to us to take care of our own business. We are all accountable for ourselves and no one else, and we are responsible for what is ours as well. Having awareness of the self is necessary on so many levels and planes on our Awakening Journey, and part of self-mastery. We can no longer allow others to define who we are, nor can they treat us as they wish. This is why we must set healthy guidelines and boundaries, for our own protection.

Knowing our worth begins with self-love and respect, first and foremost. We must see ourselves as sacred BEings aligned with the Divine and connected by our most sacred self, our spirit. We cannot go wrong when we are in true alignment with our Highest Self, living every aspect of our lives from the heart. Sure, things inevitably will not go as we planned, so we have to be able to surrender our perceived control, and allow life to happen organically, while still taking an active role in our lives and journey.

We are deserving and worthy of happiness, and a quality of life beyond who and what we were. Our happiness is a conscious choice we make every day, as is our misery and suffering. I always ask myself at the end of the day, "Did I have a bad day, or an experience I reacted to improperly?" Don't allow that perceived bad experience to ruin your happiness. We must allow ourselves to feel what we feel, but we do not have to become that emotion.

It is a part of the human condition to allow becoming what we feel, but we can work around this emotion by living from the heart, and having acceptance of the event or experience. It is our reaction and or response that we have control over, not the event or experience. This is our free will, and we have the ability to allow ourselves to not become a victim. Accept that whatever happened is fact, and respond to it from the heart. See where the opportunities are to learn, heal, and grow.

Don't allow yourself to ask, "Why is this happening?", as this puts us in survival and victim mode. When we are aligned with our heart self, the spirit, we can give love to the event and all involved with a knowing that it is temporary, that we can and must rise above it. Allow your emotions toward it to exist, find what the trigger was, and allow the healing to begin. Heal and release it with love and forgiveness, and allow love to replace your unwanted emotion. We always have choice, beginning with our perception. Change your perception, change your life and your world.

Setting healthy boundaries and sticking to them will save us from much unnecessary trouble, trauma, and pain. As I stated earlier, boundaries are meant to protect us from being put in a place by others that we are not comfortable in. We deserve to be treated respectfully and we should never allow others to be disrespectful. When setting healthy boundaries, always come from a place of love.

Calmly, yet unwavering, stand within your truth, and express your boundaries. We don't need to be defensive or threatening toward others or ourselves when drawing the line of respect. Absolutely, be firm so there is no misunderstanding, without looking down at them. Taking a perceived threat away from our intention will allow them to see we are serious without being demanding. Always come from a place of love.

Self-love and respect begin with healthy boundaries set for ourselves, and not allowing ourselves to cross the lines we have laid down. We know we have old patterns and beliefs, and when we have the recognition to replace them, we set the boundary of not allowing them to keep happening. We draw a division line of awareness and we don't allow those patterns and beliefs to exist any farther.

The awareness of their presence should bring a point of stopping our current thought process and inserting the newly desired pattern and belief. It is a process, not an event, so be gentle with yourself when inserting the new. After a while it becomes second nature and before we realize, we have changed those old ways and changed our lives for the better. This is a major part of self-mastery, assuring our evolution toward our authentic self.

Unfortunately, many of us were brought up to be people pleasers, to not "make waves," or "rock the boat," so to speak. As children, many of us were taught to be seen and not heard, and our feelings were to be ignored, to simply "do as you're told." We weren't allowed to express and when we did we were punished. Now as adults on an Awakening Journey, we realize the need to break those old patterns and beliefs projected onto us.

We never meant to be disrespectful, and still aren't, but we must speak up for ourselves and speak our truth. So much of what we were taught was incorrect, and the corrections must be made now. We can no longer live as muted children forced to live within limitations made for us. We can no longer allow ourselves to be controlled by others for their convenience, but it needs to be done respectfully. We always have choice, and it doesn't need to be conflictual in setting our boundaries.

We can no longer allow others to bully, control, and manipulate us to their way of life, conforming to a world we don't believe in.

We must live our lives for us, we must remain true to ourselves, and we must maintain our own freedom from those who would control us. We always have choice. If we can change the situation, we must. If we cannot, then we change our perception. If this is not possible, then we must let go, and often walk away.

If it is someone we must walk away from, then we simply thank them for their part on our journey, give them love and forgiveness, and go on our way, never looking back. When we reach that point of not being able to take any more, we must act and do what is necessary, but do it with love and from a place of love. We will be aligned with those meant to be in our lives, and it will constantly be an evolving door, some short-term, some long-term. Yes, sometimes we will feel pain, but we must rise above with understanding.

Jobs will be different, as we will find some we dislike that don't resonate with our purpose. We can still find happiness within that. We don't need to allow a job we feel stuck in to dampen our spirits. Hang on to it while looking for another we can exist with. I have another saying: "McDonalds is not the only place to eat." Explore all your options and choose wisely. You will be shown where you need to go. All you need to do is trust and believe that you will be given what you need, not necessarily what you want.

Protect your sacred self by all measure. Value your existence, and don't allow others to walk all over you. Don't allow others to control and manipulate you to their will and want. Love, respect, know, and value you, because you are worthy and deserving of living your life for you, and your happiness. Protect your sacred self and be true to you. You are deserving and worthy.

...Choose to live from the heart
In every aspect of your life...

Chapter 13

Empaths

What is an empath? As I researched the definition, I found many different layers to what an empath is and what their abilities are, so it will not be easy to define. I have put together a compilation of different definitions that may be helpful in understanding, although I personally feel it can be easier to understand what empaths have the ability to do.

An empath is one who, through a psychic process, has the ability to feel emotions, and feelings of not only people, animals, and other living things, but inanimate objects as well. I know it's vague, and I believe the definition goes much deeper than I can begin to explain. All sentient beings are empaths, so it does not mean we are special or have a "superpower".

Empaths are gifted in many different ways of feeling and sensing energy, which is what we do. We see, feel, and have a certain knowing of energy, and are able to translate into words and images the feelings from these traits. Everyone has the ability to feel and sense energy and more. Some of us have nurtured these gifts and allowed them to become much more than just sensing.

We have progressed into intuitives, psychics, mediums, channels, and so many other labels spirituality gives us. All of us are born with these abilities, while some don't have awareness until later in life, and others never really are aware of these gifts, perhaps because it is not a part of their journey.

As with any gift we have been given, it all begins with an awareness. I say we are given gifts, because we don't own them, and they are not exclusive to us alone as we all have the ability, so it doesn't make us special and above others. With awareness, many feel confused as they have no understanding of this new part of themselves, so they choose to ignore it and deny its existence. They are denying their own reality, and that is their choice, but in the end, we cannot deny who or what we are. Choosing to be aware of our empathic abilities will allow us to nurture them.

To develop our gifts, we choose to be aware each time we have an experience, and we allow ourselves to pay attention to how it makes us feel, and recognize that we did have an experience. Constantly recognizing the experiences allows us to nurture them, and we become more attuned to the vibrations and we improve our abilities.

Now that we have accepted this as a part of us, there is a natural progression that will follow as we grow. We really begin to see synchronicities and begin to see the world in a much different way. Many feel as if the world they believe they know is changing. The world isn't changing... you are. As we allow our perception to change, we may feel suddenly as if we are lost, we feel something is wrong with us, and many will see their immediate world crash around them, and begin to feel helpless and out of control.

The feelings of being different and abnormal, and self-doubt will consume some of us, and frighten us away from our reality, and again, we deny our own existence. Many will be afraid to talk with anyone about their experiences, and feel they need to hide their gifts in fear of how others will perceive us, pushing ourselves into a state of becoming a hermit, totally hiding from society.

This misunderstanding that they are the only ones gifted is tragic, since we all are born with these abilities. Not knowing where to go and feeling as if no one understands them, they end up suffering needlessly, as many of us do. Accepting ourselves unconditionally will break us free of any suffering we bring ourselves.

I assure you, when you embrace yourself and your gifts, you'll find a freedom few experience, and see the beauty in who you are and what you are capable of. Once embraced, the world is indeed different. Some will see the ugly truth of life and allow themselves to become controlled by that fear, becoming its slave, while others who see the truths will separate from it and allow their own freedom. It is a choice we all will make at some point.

Balance in anything is essential in life and something we all must strive for in every aspect of our lives. Empathy is a part of us all and we need to become comfortable and accept this part of us.

Allowing ourselves to be who we are authentically will help bring that balance we seek.

We all will feel vulnerable to some degree, and uncomfortable in situations, and we don't know how to respond to our feelings. Often in close proximity of others we feel unexplainable discomfort, we feel a need to leave immediately, and we may become dizzy and feel sick to our stomach.

This is your gift sensing the energy of someone or something nearby. When we feel this, we need to pay close attention to our immediate surrounding and pinpoint where it is coming from. Stay as long as you can and allow yourself to focus on those closest to you.

Feel their energy and gauge your response. This is known as your intuition or gut feeling. This is something you should become well acquainted with, as it will serve you well the rest of your life, and could indeed save your life or someone close by. Trust this intuition and study it closely.

What do you sense from the person you're focusing on? Do this with each person near you, but do it without letting them know this is what you are doing. This is how we nurture our gifts, by "practicing" and paying close attention to it. We consciously and knowingly feel into or read others and their energy. The best place to focus on are someone's eyes, and we can do this with pictures as well.

I have helped many others through the use of pictures to nurture their gifts, and practiced this way personally for years, honing and improving them. Get with someone you know, have them show you pictures of someone they know well, and really study the picture.

Start saying what you are feeling and what you see in their eyes and have them tell you if you are right or wrong. Don't get discouraged if you're wrong more than right, as this is telling you your perception needs adjusting. It also allows you to gauge your senses, when you are right as opposed to wrong, and how each feels to you. This is also learning to trust yourself.

Keep doing this and eventually you'll begin to trust your intuition and yourself with confidence. Take this into the real world and keep doing it with live people. You will begin to see others as they truly are, you'll begin to see other things about them as well. As your gifts progress and improve you may begin to notice that you know things about them.

Many of us are now beginning to think perhaps we're not just an empath. Many of us will evolve our gifts into what they truly are, manifesting in psychic abilities, mediums, intuitives, etc. Some of us can see the future of others, their past in this life and past lives, some of us learn we can see their spirit and communicate with it, and some of us are able to see into the body and find medical issues.

If we allow ourselves to evolve, many of us find we have multiple gifts and can see and feel some truly amazing things. Being an empath is so much more than what spirituality has defined for us and unfortunately limits our belief in who we truly are. When we fully accept and realize our unlocked potential, and dedicate to our gifts and nurture them, a whole new world of possibilities opens up to us.

Many ancient civilizations, as well as extraterrestrial civilizations, have the ability to communicate telepathically, and our species does have this ability if we just allow it to be. We are constantly being bombarded with energies from the Universe that are allowing us to evolve within our extra sensory perceptions and fields.

One of the most important things we can do for ourselves in ensuring our evolution, not only with our gifts but on our Awakening journey, is to trust and believe in ourselves. We must have an inner knowing that we are capable of much more than we realize, and that we in fact are limitless.

The institutions we have been taught to trust have set limits upon us and we, as children, were made to believe we could only do so much within our existence, so we feel comfortable living within the box of limits they gave us. Giving ourselves permission to transcend all limits projected upon us, not only allows our evolution, it allows us to believe and trust in ourselves. We, as empaths, need to be free of all constructs and limitations.

We don't really have a choice when our gifts begin to manifest, and many will try to ignore them because we have been taught it isn't natural to be this way. Religion would like us to believe they come from "Satan" and are indeed evil manifestations, so we shame ourselves and try and convince ourselves we are evil. This is in an effort to control the masses by means of fear of not being "normal".

The church knew centuries ago we all possess the abilities of all the expanded senses and that they are indeed natural. The church would label us "witches" because we became a threat, thinking outside the fears they projected onto us. That projection of fear has been ingrained in our DNA throughout time and is unfortunate in its judgment.

Shamans, druids, and medicine men embraced these gifts and were considered "Holy Men/Women" by their tribes, and were sought out for their higher dimensional knowledge. They have been with us since the beginnings of our civilization, only there were fewer then because the earth was not as heavily populated as it is today.

They were highly regarded, often being the ones educated, and if there was a written language could read and write, and this would later transfer to monks and priests after religions were organized, or only allowed by the aristocratic society. This set them above all others and gave them a sense of being privileged.

These gifted individuals were often the ones who made the local laws, settled disputes, and had rituals for just about any situation, including fertility, rain, and drought, casting their spells, as it was their responsibility to communicate with the gods and deities the commoners worshipped. They were in fact, regarded as being more important and powerful than the chieftains and tribal elders.

They were to be feared yet respected because of their awareness of a higher knowledge and how it related to everyday life. They were astrologers and astronomers following the moon and sun cycles and would decide when to plant and harvest crops, when to propagate the species, sacrifices to their gods, and other necessary rituals to maintain a balanced life.

Unfortunately, if life became difficult, perhaps a drought, or too much rain, diseased crops, deformed children, defeat in war, they were the ones to take the blame, and subsequently paid with their lives because nature didn't respond as they thought she should. And the cycle would continue with another holy person and there was a new found hope and all was well. It was known, that those who communed with a higher energy should be revered and celebrated, often worshipped, often feared.

As tribes were absorbed into a larger society, there was a need to control the population through a hierarchy, and the common man was denigrated to the status of slave, servant, and in many societies, animals. Unfortunately, not much has changed and the common man is still treated as they were thousands of years ago, to maintain control by the world leaders and elite. Genocide still happens in our modern world through an even more sinister ethnic cleansing through religious beliefs.

Today, with scientific advancement, we are controlled with man-made chemicals in our food, drink, and liquid to keep us stupid and weak, dependent on our governments, making us believe we should fear and obey them. Having the awareness, as most empaths do, many of us gravitate to conspiracy theories, which are distractions away from our journey to authenticity.

It is that same scientific and mathematical process that the gifted and ways of our etheric existence are being accepted into mainstream beliefs. Thanks to the genius minds of Plato, Socrates, Newton, Einstein, and Tesla, to name a few, the metaphysical world has been proven to exist. The spiritual world is slowly becoming accepted by society, and we are not regarded as mutant enigmas, made to seem degenerates.

Through the use of computers, the internet, and social media we have the ability to reference and answer any question we may have to educate ourselves, and accept ourselves as "normal" beings. But with this ability, we all must learn to use discernment from what is fact and what is spiritual mythology. We simply cannot take it as truth just because we saw it on social media.

Getting back to the modern empaths and those of us with heightened senses, we now have opportunity to bring understanding instead of fear of our gifts. We know now that we are not alone, and in fact, many others have also been where we are. We can learn to accept what we are and become comfortable in that acceptance.

We can learn how to nurture our gifts and allow them to become what they truly are, with great understanding. As we become the gifted empath, most of us will feel the need to heal, save, or help others and feel it is our responsibility. But why do we feel we need to? Why do we feel it is our responsibility? *Why am I the one who is going to help that person?*

Many of us grew up in dysfunctional families, perhaps with a narcissist or controlling parent, with verbal, mental, and physical abuse. Our childhood in many cases was stolen from us, our innocence was taken from us, and we are left with deep wounds and scars and no Idea how to move beyond it all. Although we are products of our childhood, we are accountable for who we are as adults.

Many of us were shamed, belittled, made to feel extreme guilt, and grew up confused and not liking ourselves very much. Most of us, even in our adult lives, can't love ourselves, because we never healed our childhood, and still don't like ourselves. Many of us still feel inferior, because we were made to feel less than those who raised us, and that enigma, that need to fix those who raised us, is a major reason why we need to save, help, and heal others. By helping others, we are, in a roundabout way, trying to heal our past and ourselves.

We feel as if our guardians were broken, because even as children we were empaths, often being told we are too sensitive, cried too much, and made to believe we were weak. They couldn't understand us because we didn't fit into their perception of how they wanted us to be.

We grow up playing the victim to our upbringing and, somehow, we will fix it and make it right. The only way to make all of that right is to connect with the inner child and allow them to show us where and what needs to be healed. Our guardians did the best they could, but as adults, we have to clean up the mess they created and that is no easy task.

You don't have to remember the physical pain, just the emotional pain. Many of our triggers came during our childhood development, so that's where we need to start. Sometimes as an adult empath, our need to help others is actually us reaching out for the help we believe we are giving. We aren't really helping them, we're helping ourselves.

As healers we know that as we heal others, we are healing ourselves. Many feel that by helping others, we can justify our existence by comparing our lives to theirs. In some twisted way of thinking, by comparing our life to other's lives, we can also feel good about our own life. In the psychology world, needing to save and heal others is referred to as a "Messiah or Christ complex". We feel we are the ones meant to save and help others, and that it is therefore our responsibility.

It has never been, nor will it ever be our responsibility to heal or even change others. None of us came here specifically to take responsibility for what others need to fix within their lives and on their journey. We have enough to take care of within ourselves, and that is where our focus should lie, not in the journey of others.

We, having the ability to feel the emotions of others, cannot take on their emotions and make them ours. Just because someone projects their emotional baggage, does not mean we have to accept it. There is no way possible for us to take care of our own 3D self, while our focus is on fixing others. It takes way too much energy and pulls us away from our own journey inward.

Indeed, we can have empathy and concern, and we can offer help and healing, but we must think about the probability that they are on a much different journey, and our efforts to save and heal may in fact be counterproductive to their journey, and we have become, in our innocent intention, controlling. We walk many fine lines on our journey.

Many of those we feel we must help are not here on an Awakening or healing journey, but we can plant seeds. How they choose to nurture those seeds is not our business, as they are on their journey, not ours, and we all must allow and respect the journey and truths of others, without judgement. We must also allow them to be who they are. Again, we are risking being controlling.

It is not our responsibility to tell others their beliefs are wrong because they are different from ours. One of our birthrights is to believe without the persecution of others who do not agree with us. This is what is referred to as "spiritual ego" in believing our truth is absolute, and any opposing our thought or belief is wrong.

Many of us having a newfound awareness of our Awakening or spiritual journeys are still being led by the wounded ego, as we have not yet learned to live from our heart-centered self, the spirit. We are so taken by this new trend in thought, and some believe they have been told by "God Himself" that only their belief is right.

Only through using discernment can we fully understand that what we read on social media, is an opinion of others being led by their wounded ego as well. Although it may seem as though we resonate with what they say, it is a perspective. One surefire way around this is to research those who have withstood the test of time in their truth.

We cannot allow ourselves to be led by what has become "spiritual mythology" within the fad of spirituality that social media presents to us. Just like anything else we want to know about, we must take the time to properly arm ourselves with fact and not theories. Our Awakening Journey is within, toward a higher truth, not opinion. "I read it on the internet so it must be true". Not by a long shot.

Imagine what our world would be like if doctors, lawyers, psychologists, pharmacists, veterinarians, etc., learned their trade from social media and not accepted higher learning platforms. It is no different than spirituality and Awakening in the necessity for higher learning and not theory or opinion. Engage your higher self and those who are authentic leaders in this search for knowledge and wisdom.

The Awakening Journey is incredibly complex, on may planes of existence and most of those on an etheric level, and is meant to bring us out of the 3D and into the authentic self, the spirit. There are many newfound empaths who believe, because of what they encounter on social media, that we can manifest and attract whatever we want or desire. This is also spiritual mythology.

We contracted for our very existence before we incarnated and all that goes with that existence, therefore, just because we want something, doesn't entitle us to it. We will always be given what we need, not necessarily what we want. The spiritual and Awakening Journey is of the spirit and not the material, and the focus is meant to be exactly that.

There is no harm at all in desiring to better our standing in life, but many who follow the spiritual fad believe they are deserving of material gain to better our spiritual self. Our true essence is not what we possess on this journey, but who we are within our journey. How many times have you seen someone cross over to the spirit world and actually take possessions with them?

When our body expires, and it will, we return to our spirit self, and what we actually take with us into the next incarnation is what we have learned, healed, and evolved. Personally, I believe I will spend my life with this focus in mind. When we read our Akashic Record, we will be able to see exactly what we contracted for, and what we achieved toward fulfilling those contracts.

Unfortunately for some of us, we will see our Akash and realize truths we may not want to see. For many of us, it is multiple lifetimes of allowing the same lessons to go unlearned, and for some of us, we find the 3D self chooses not to fulfill those contracts lifetime after lifetime. We had a saying where I used to work, "…you always have time to do it right the second time…".

Chapter 14

Transitioning

Transitioning is an often-used word in spirituality and Awakening Journeys, but what does it mean exactly from our point of view? The dictionary defines transition as 1a: passage from one state, stage, subject, or place to another: change – 1b: a movement, development, or evolution from one form, stage, or style to another. I need to make some modifications to their definition to fit within the energy of our process.

When we experience the many transitions on our journeys, we are stepping out of the current phase into a new, stronger, and higher phase. Our journey is in an upward and forward spiraling motion much like our galaxy moving through the cosmos. I use the term "phase" instead of "level" as level implies a series of tests or advancement criteria from one to the next, whereas phase is a continuation of process.

Tests imply pass/fail criteria and only limited movement, based on expectation of completion. We are never tested by the Divine, but by our perception, guided by a societal need of measuring "knowledge" through the educational norm. Our journeys are indigenous to the self, as we all have our own pace of evolution, and not a mass sense of accomplishment, passing through rigorous testing.

We all will experience what our spirit self needs and we cannot compare our journey to that of others. Unfortunately, we are taught at an early age to compare our personal achievements, in maintaining a false sense of being better than another or risk being seen as lesser than another. The higher our grade, the smarter we are, is what we are taught to believe.

This could not be any farther from truth in reality. There are many forms of "smart" and "intelligence", but our projected competitive need to surpass that of others has only led to an overblown ego and a false sense of a hierarchy. There is no positioning of better or less than any other, as we are all uniquely different to begin with.

This false sense brings entitlement and a sense of authority, which do not exist when one speaks in matters of the spirit. Since we all come from the same source it is impossible for one to be either greater or less than another, but that does not make us all equal either. We cannot be equal as we are on different parts of our journey and there can be no comparisons made as to "what level" we are on. The process is a constant continuation, and therefore, we simply move from one phase to another without any marked accomplishment criteria.

With this different perception of transition, we can now allow upward and forward movement without the need to control our journey, thus allowing it to be as it is meant to be, not how we believe it should be. We will endure many emotional pains and traumas, an incredible amount of uncertainty, and a sense of feeling lost and insecure.

These feelings are referred to as "vulnerability", and as uncomfortable as it is and will be, it is the only state of BEing we can grow spiritually and personally within. We have lost all sense of what we were, believed, thought, or knew. It is our "unbecoming" of all that was projected onto us from birth, and into our spirit self, our true identity.

As we evolve into a higher version of ourselves, our truth has to evolve with us. We are no longer who we were, and what we knew as truth from one phase to another has no choice but to change with us. The idea that we must hold our truth as absolute is presented from the wounded ego and its needing to know what God knows, declaring only our perception is right.

This sense of being elevated above others is instilled in us from a young age through the institutions we were guided by. The outdated use of tests in the education system has told us that those who know all the answers to the tests are smarter, and therefore, should be held in a higher sense of esteem, and looked up to. In truth, it only shows an ability to remember information and knowledge, not wisdom.

Since we all develop at different rates and ways, some with incredible intelligence may not advance until later in life. It doesn't mean they are stupid or less intelligent, it simply means we all are on different places on our journey. Some of us are older souls which have been in existence quite a long time, and some of us are younger souls coming into existence more recently.

Those souls who have been in existence longer have more experiences to draw upon than younger souls, and have the ability to use that wisdom in many positive ways. They possess a different range of understanding and know they are not of a higher standing, unless they are being ruled by the wounded ego. Spiritual ego has been the downfall of many not living their Divine path, and they will see as such when they read their Akashic Record upon their final transition.

Each of us will experience our transitions as we are meant to when we allow it to be organic. Many of us, though, will experience as our ego directs us to, taking away from the reality of our transitions. This is one of the main reasons we need to heal and balance our wounded ego, as it works to keep us locked in the comfort zone it has created for us.

There will be many with shared experiences quite similar to the masses, and we can help each other through these rough periods if we remain open. Many will see "symptoms" just like everyone else but aren't able to step out of survival or victim modes. This resistance to a naturally occurring process will only bring unnecessary suffering and pain. Again, as I have stated any times here, see opportunity to learn, heal, and grow and stop asking "why is this happening to me".

Allowing ourselves to be open to the inevitable changes coming, will afford us an opportunity to glide more easily through what could be a traumatic experience. Change your perspective and change your life. Allow yourself to flow with what is happening, allow your spirit self to guide you, and trust that when you come out on the other side, life will be incredibly different. Embrace the uncertainty of inevitable change.

I often hear others speak of how hard it is to transition. Indeed, it is because change itself is not easy. The process of transitioning is that of great change, again, the unbecoming of our former self, becoming our authentic self, the spirit. I can't stress enough how invaluable and important awareness and recognition of the self is. This knowing of the self, through self-mastery, allows us a deeper understanding of this process.

In order to know who we are, we must understand who we've been and why. This inward journey of Awakening will take us through this lifetime, as well as past lifetimes, to find the root of who we are, and who we aren't. Often times, it's easier to determine who we aren't to separate who we desire to be, as opposed to who we truly are. This is no easy task, but one we must undertake to assure our evolution.

This determination can be quite awkward and uncomfortable as we sift through our emotional baggage, discarding the projections of others toward us, with the remainder being ours to own. I personally know this process can be painstaking and arduous, but this is the process of self-mastery and how we perform it. It's no different than the process of defragmenting and deleting the hard drive on our computer.

This process is along the lines of using a fishbone chart used in many business applications. It is a system of "if, if then, else, if then else" etc. If we can visualize these steps, it will become easier to recognize what is ours and what is not. We delete what is no longer needed, making room for what is and will be needed. This purge creates space for what serves us and our highest good.

This process is expansive in many areas in our life and we find ourselves multitasking several processes simultaneously. The actual hardest part of this process is choosing to make the mindset to allow the process to proceed. The ego will fight this process because it has no desire to change, creating inner conflict and the perception of a deeper degree of difficulty. It is not ours to ignore or do away with the pesky ego, rather to heal and balance it.

We can't shut down the ego as it is an integral part of us, and we certainly can't treat it as a child acting out and placing it in a corner either. We must nurture it with love and compassion and bring it the understanding it lacks, much as we would a child. The ego is, after all, at the development stage of a child, and will need to be taught from an Awakening perspective to bring the balance and healing necessary.

I know this all sounds complicated, and it is, but once we allow ourselves to step into self-discipline with confidence, we can and will achieve our Divine outcome. Change is never easy to accept, but the degree of difficulty will be determined based on acceptance of the importance of allowing change. This acceptance is far beyond a simple basic need. It's urgent.

Transitioning from one phase to the next, is in itself, evolution. I know quite well that the most difficult phase of transitioning is the final phase because it's all coming together in one final push. We often speak of peaks and valleys, or highs and lows. This final stage is where we come to the peak of the inner turbulence and conflict, releasing all we have experienced through the process of transition.

When we climb a hill or mountain, we are aware of the difficulty as we journey to the top. It is, in a sense, achieving a personal goal. As we come closer to the top, we feel a sense of urgency with excitement as we look back and see how far we have come, realizing we don't have as far to go. Our transition is much the same way. We're weary and tired, frustrated and burnt out, but we know if we stop now, we won't achieve our goal. What's important to remember is to not look forward to see how far we have to go, but to look back to see how far we have come, and to see our triumphs.

It is, after all, about the journey and not the destination that is of importance. As we look back, we understand we can't stay in that past, as it's no longer where we are or who we are. Look back in remembrance and gratitude for the opportunities to learn, heal, and grow, and give ourselves reassurance that we have been through some incredibly rough times, and survived, and learned to thrive.

As we reach the pinnacle of transition, we realize a sense of being able to breathe and relax for a short time, with the understanding life has leveled off for a moment. During this period, we may find that we can't feel our energy, guides, or Divinity. I assure you; they are still there and quite active. The transition has brought us to a new and higher level of frequency.

It will take us some time to adjust to this new and elevated frequency and begin to "feel" again. Take this time to go deeper within to allow that newness to come forward and present itself. We can't force energy, as that sets blocks and makes it harder than it needs to be. Simply enjoy the "spiritual vacation", or downtime we have been given.

Allow yourself the time for this readjustment period without putting unnecessary pressure on ourselves through constant doubt of the self. It's imperative to be compassionate and loving of the self as we allow our transitions to be organic. I can't stress enough not trying to force anything on our journey, as it only blocks us from what is meant to be.

We don't have to understand everything we're going through. Most of it is on the etheric level, not the 3D. Staying out of our head and living a heart-based existence will serve us well, allowing ourselves to be guided by the spirit self as we leave our 3D led life. Living from the heart in every aspect of our lives alleviates unnecessary hardship through trust and acceptance.

As we have come to the end of our transition, we may find signs from our new spirit guides, and realization of familiar guides exiting our lives. This transition brings a new purpose and the old guides have finished their purpose, allowing the new guides for our new purpose. We don't have a singular purpose, rather a series when one has been accomplished. The transition brings an end and beginning to our lives, continuing the circle of life.

Perhaps our new guides will introduce themselves by means of personal gifts, such as smell, visions, dreams, or other means. Our awareness of these signs is them letting us know of their existence. Welcome them with an open heart. Ask them if they can give us their name. They won't always, as sometimes it's not necessary, or we simply can't pronounce it.

Know without a doubt they are here to guide us on this next phase of purpose and will remain with us until they have finished their purpose. Always give gratitude with love to our exiting guides for all they have done for us. Many of them have gone above and beyond their contract to make sure we have done what is necessary.

Quite frankly, I know first-hand, some of my guides are exhausted and overwhelmed by all they had to do to ensure my evolution. Our 3D self can be quite a problem for them at times, not wanting to cooperate and do what is needed. They earned their place in our hearts and deserve our deepest gratitude, and sometimes our most heartfelt apologies. They have purpose just like us, and when they have been successful, they move onto their next purpose.

Transition is never easy, but that doesn't mean it has to be difficult. Remembering to always allow what is meant to be — not what we want — we can make these transitions easier, avoiding self-imposed trauma and suffering.

Personally, one of the hardest lessons I have had to learn was to not be my own worst enemy. Our 3D selves have a tendency to overcomplicate and sabotage our journey because we allow our journey to be led by the wounded ego, and not the spirit self. There are many phases to our Awakening Journey, and we must allow it to be organic and not forced by the ego.

Take all of these processes done simultaneously, and we can begin to see ourselves in a new light and perception, with a deeper realization and understanding of how magnificent we truly are.

The miracles and magic we look for from the outside world have always been within us. It is only with trust and belief in the self that we can unbecome our former projected self, and become our authentic self.

Heal well, journey well.

There is no greater gift

We can give to ourself

Than unconditional love,

And total acceptance

Of our own inner Divinity.

Notes

Notes